If Trees Could Speak

If Trees Could Speak

STORIES OF AUSTRALIA'S GREATEST TREES

BOB BEALE

ALLEN&UNWIN

First published in 2007
Copyright text © Bob Beale 2007
Copyright photography © Bob Beale 2007 unless otherwise stated

Allen & Unwin
83 Alexander Street
Crows Nest NSW 2065
Australia
Phone: (61 2) 8425 0100
Fax: (61 2) 9906 2218
Email: info@allenandunwin.com
Web: www.allenandunwin.com

National Library of Australia
Cataloguing-in-Publication entry:

Beale, Bob.
    If trees could speak: stories of Australia's greatest trees.

    1st ed.
    Bibliography.
    Includes index.
    ISBN 978 1 74114 276 1 (pbk.)

    1. Trees - Australia. 2. Historic trees - Australia I.
    Title.

    582.160994

Edited by Rosanne Fitzgibbon
Cover design by Phil Campbell
Text designed and typeset by Phil Campbell
Printed in China through Colorcraft Ltd, Hong Kong
10 9 8 7 6 5 4 3 2 1

To my grandson, Liam:
I have planted an ironbark for him
– may they both grow strong and true.

Contents

Preface

Some of my fondest boyhood memories are of sitting on a branch of a big tree in our front yard. Many happy hours were spent clambering up it, swinging like Tarzan, hanging upside down, or pretending I was in a castle, in the jungle or on a mountain. Playground equipment had nothing on this. Sometimes I dared myself to venture into the danger zone of slender branches, to rob a bird's nest or rescue a stranded kite.

The trunk forked near the ground for a handy foothold which, in turn, led to a thick limb that rose gently upward. Monkeying up on all fours I came to a level section; with one arm wrapped around a vertical branch, I could sit there safely. It was hard on the bum but the solidity of it was reassuring. A bonus was that you could spy on the passing parade on the footpath below. Undetected, I could stare in a way not deemed polite for a kid down there on terra firma. The tree also provided a steady supply of ants, bugs and other critters to educate me about which ones had stings and which could be tormented with impunity. Most of all, it was just pleasant to sit up there, swinging my legs and daydreaming. A clean, sappy scent wafted around and I could smell the bark on my hands. When the wind blew, the tree would toss its head and sigh, swaying like a ship at anchor. I pitied kids raised in apartments or overbuilt housing blocks with no place for a decent-sized tree.

During the writing of this book, many people told me similar fond memories of a tree they associated with a place, a person or a special time in their lives. In the same way a certain fragrance can transport you straight back to your grandmother's house, or a favourite sweater you once owned, or your local bakery. Nostalgia about trees evokes a more visual kind of memory. We associate the trees of our childhood with being active and carefree.

I wrote to one of Australia's foremost botanists, now retired, and asked him to single out an individual tree that he personally regarded as having national significance. Like many others, he singled out the Burke and Wills Dig Tree in Queensland. Second on his list was the Separation Tree in the Royal Botanic Gardens, Melbourne. He said if he could nominate species, his chart-toppers would be the river red gum, the coolibah 'about which we all sing', and possibly the Wollemi pine. I smiled when I read his final choice: 'For me, the jacaranda in the backyard at Mum's where I learnt to climb and sit and think was a very special tree.'

I hope this book will promote a greater appreciation of the trees that are special to us all collectively as Australians. They are as much part of us and our history as the heritage buildings, the great artworks, the books and precious artefacts we conserve in our museums, yet we often fail to value them.

Any traveller can use this book as the inspiration for an extended journey around the continent, with these outstanding trees as guideposts. The information will lead foreign visitors onto unusual trails of inquiry, offering unique insights into Australia and Australians. It will take you to many wonderful places to see unforgettable sights. In time, perhaps each city will develop its own heritage-tree trail. A national trail linking them all would be a remarkable attraction. The innovative Tree Tops Walk in the Valley of the Giants near Walpole, in Western Australia, has attracted almost two million visitors since it opened in 1996. The nearby Gloucester Tree is Pemberton's most famous tourist attraction, visited by 400 000 people a year. You can climb 60 metres up this giant karri to take in the forest at canopy level from a former bushfire watchtower. In 2002, the millionth person braved the white-knuckled climb up the spiral ladder of metal pegs embedded into its sturdy trunk. Many of us, it seems, are still kids at heart.

Bob Beale
Faculty of Science
University of New South Wales, Sydney

Introduction

Among all the varied productions with which nature has adorned the surface of the earth, none awakens our sympathies, or interests our imagination so powerfully as those venerable trees which seem to have withstood the lapse of ages – silent witnesses of the successive generations of man, to whose destiny they bear so touching a resemblance, alike in their budding, their prime and their decay.

Jacob Strutt

Australia's story is written in trees. You can read its ancient origins in the cool mystical Antarctic beech forests of the south and in the vibrant green rainforests of the north. The tale of its long slow drift into drought and fire is imprinted in the black furrowed bark of the brigalow, the stunted mallee, the miserly mulga and the leathery hang-dog leaves of the gums. Trees are deeply ingrained in our human history as well, the stuff of everything from cricket stumps and goalposts to shearing sheds and surfboats. More than any other product of nature, trees gave us the raw material to build, shape and express what we are as a nation. They remain central to our daily lives, our character and hopes: they are literally at the root of our national identity.

Foreign trees supplied the wooden hulls, decks, spars and masts of the sailing ships that brought Dutch, Portuguese and British explorers and, eventually, the colonists and convicts of the First Fleet. When the Union Jack was hoisted for the first time at the head of Sydney Cove on 26 January 1788, it was a casuarina that held it aloft. A week later, the arched canopy of a great spreading tree – perhaps a Port Jackson fig – became the make-do church where troops and convicts joined Reverend Richard Johnson to celebrate the first Christian thanksgiving on Australian soil. Soon the Fatal

Facing page: A myrtle tree in the rainforest at Mount Anne in southwest Tasmania, photographed by Peter Dombrovskis in 1984.

5

Tree was pressed into service on the colony's dark side: when Australia's first criminal court convicted four convicts of theft, they were hanged from one of its stout limbs. In the space of just one month, trees were central players in the foundation of the state, the church and the law. Sadly, all three – and many others with starring roles in the birth of the nation – were later felled and lost to history.

Native hardwoods provided the shingles and boards for the settlers' roofs, walls and floors, and the fuel for warmth and cooking. They made the stockades for convict road gangs, the timbers of the paddock fences, the mustering yards and the farmhouses from which the colony rode to prosperity on the sheep's back. Legions of red cedar, blue gum and swamp mahogany fell to the axe to make everything from exquisite furniture to the hulking great wool stores and wharves that were the gateways for prosperous trade.

Trees were vital to early settlers

Trees provided the wagons, wheels, tool handles and pit-props that helped the gold rush jolt the fledgling economy into life. They were the bonfire in which the Ballarat gold-diggers burnt their licences; the bloodied planks of the Eureka stockade; the sturdy poles for the Overland Telegraph; the vertebral sleepers of our great railway lines; the source of the tannins that preserved leather boots and saddles; the medicinal oils that cleansed wounds and cleared blocked noses; the paper for newsprint and the books that recorded our stories and promulgated our laws; the timbers of the grim gallows that hanged Ned Kelly; and the countless rough-hewn posts for the Dingo Fence . . . the list is as long as that fence.

Trees are embedded in the symbols of our national identity: our green and gold national sporting colours represent the leaves and cheerful pompom blossoms of the wattle tree, which also underpins our coat of arms with a branch in bloom fanned out like a lyrebird's tail beneath the crest.

In our most famous song, 'Waltzing Matilda', the coolibah shelters the sheep-stealing swaggie – one shady character as silent witness to another. Eucalypts inspired May Gibbs's fanciful children's stories of Snugglepot and Cuddlepie, Bib and Bub and the Gumnut Babies. They are there in our vernacular, in colourful phrases such

as 'hard as ironbark', 'up a gum tree' and 'beyond the black stump', or describing places like mallee country, out in the mulga, a paperbark swamp or the brigalow scrub. Their names are as distinctly Australian as the trees themselves – kurrajong, wilga, gidgee, illyarrie and karri – and colourfully evoke something of their character – blue-leaved stringy-bark, woolly butt, sand-dune bloodwood, scribbly gum and Kimberley yellow jacket.

Australia's eucalypts have a unique character

Hans Heysen, Fred Williams, Arthur Boyd and many other artists have used native trees as identifiers and sentinels in their landscapes. The 1988 edition of Manning Clark's classic *A Short History of Australia* has endpapers featuring a crowded gum-tree forest, a 'detail of Sydney Nolan's painting *Riverbend*, a celebration of the golden tree of life'. A number of trees painted from life in colonial times still stand, long after the artists themselves have returned to the soil. The same is true of many trees that feature

Introduction

in fiction, music and public life.

The Shepparton house and shed where Joseph Furphy wrote the Aussie classic *Such is Life* are long gone, but the tousle-headed wilga tree, the lovely 'Australian willow' he planted, still thrives there. It's a signpost by which to find your way into his lost world of bullockies, kerosene lamps and billy tea stirred with a eucalyptus twig. Furphy's words live on, too, as in this eloquent passage from his novel:

> Mary O'Halloran was perfect Young-Australian . . . a very creature of the phenomena which had environed her own dawning intelligence. She was a child of the wilderness, a dryad among her kindred trees. The long-descended poetry of her nature made the bush vocal with pure gladness of life; endowed each tree with sympathy, respondent to her own fellowship. She had noticed the dusky aspect of the ironwood; the volumed cumuli of rich olive-green crowning the lordly currajong; the darker shade of the wilga's messy foliage-cataract; the clearer tint of the tapering pine; the clean-spotted column of the leopard tree, creamy white on slate, from base to topmost twig. She pitied the unlovely belar, when the wind sighed through its coarse, scanty, grey-green tresses; and she loved to contemplate the silvery plumage of the two drooping myalls which, because of their rarity here, had been allowed to remain in the horse-paddock. For the last two or three springs of her vivacious existence, she had watched the deepening crimson of the quondong, amidst its thick contexture of Nile-green leaves; she had marked the unfolding bloom of the scrub, in its many-hued beauty; she had revelled in the audacious black-and-scarlet glory of the desert pea. She knew the dwelling-place of every loved companion; and, by necessity, she had her own names for them all.

Our strange and wonderful native trees give the whole Australian landscape its unique appearance and feel: the lofty gums of the towering southern forests with their raw-boned elbows, gangling limbs and festoons of bark; the eerie ghost gums of the arid centre, perfect in their powdery whiteness; the contorted snow gums of the high mountain country; the stern, claw-footed red gums standing guard on inland riverbanks; the beer-bellied boabs and bottle trees of the north; the massed ranks of soaring karri and jarrah in the south-west; and the solid-liquid buttresses of the rainforest figs, with their fluted butts and waxy roots slithering across the rocks.

A few precious old trees, some right in the heart of our cities today, bear witness to not-so-long-departed Aboriginal people and their relationships with trees. One may reveal where a soft cradle for a baby was carefully sliced from a fat paperbark, or a huge scar on a river red gum shows where the bark for a canoe was hacked with stone axes, or another tree shows footholds cut by an agile climber searching for a native 'sugarbag' beehive to rob of its sweet honey.

Early European explorers on the continent's west coast and in Tasmania did not find gold, silver or spices but they did find trees that delighted them. Willem de Vlamingh came in 1696 in search of a Dutch trading ship lost two years earlier. He didn't find it, but he did land on Dirk Hartog Island and find the pewter plate left there, nailed to a post (there were no trees), by Hartog in 1616. When a landing party went ashore on Rottnest Island on 31 December 1696, de Vlamingh noted in his log: 'After breakfast I went ashore with our bookkeeper and sent our longboat ashore with a party of hands to cut firewood which was to be had there in abundance and very fine of fragrance just like rosewood, of which I have had some in our own boat full taken on board . . .' The explorers were using native sandalwood, which now fetches many thousands of dollars a tonne for its beautiful scented oil, to burn as fuel.

The dwindling band of ancient native trees still living within sight of our major cities is emblematic of our near-total destruction of the natural landscape. Australia's oldest surviving exotic tree, a wizened olive planted in 1805 by John Macarthur, serves as a living reminder of the transplanted European culture that swept aside Aboriginal culture along with native plants and animals alike.

An early dawning of awareness of the virtues of native flora and fauna, and adaptation to local realities, is there in Governor Macquarie's choice for Australia's first street trees in 1815: a short but sweet avenue of swamp mahoganies in Sydney's Botanic Gardens that probably were the first formal planting of a native species. Some of those same trees survive to this day.

Trees recorded the coded symbols of the age of exploration

We use trees to remember our history. The Dig Tree and others like it with their coded symbols embody an age of discovery, courage, foolhardiness, victory and failure in the nineteenth century. The Tree of Knowledge at Barcaldine in Queensland

Introduction

marks the political birth of blue-collar workers. Many a tree planted ceremonially by a visiting official commemorates an important date or event. Memorial avenues dotted around Victoria and Western Australia are a uniquely Australian expression of grief. More than any other, perhaps, the Lone Pine merits a special place of honour among the memorials. Although not a native, its direct ties to the horrors of war and Gallipoli are palpable reminders of those who suffered for the common good. It tells us, too, that life goes on.

Other trees embody our extraordinary natural heritage. Many are living history books of a time before European settlement. Huon pines in Tasmania predate the birth of Christ, and other trees are far more ancient still. The rare red cabbage palms of Palm Valley reveal a distant age when Central Australia was not desert but rainforest. Albert Namatjira's paintbrush captured the ancient spirit, the graceful stems and flickering light-play of these beautiful palms, as well as the haunting ghost gums and hardy bloodwoods of the red centre. His evocative images gave Australians fresh eyes to see the rich, vibrant beauty of their arid heartland.

The discovery of the Wollemi Pine, the botanical equivalent of finding a living dinosaur, not only astonished us but gave us a powerful feeling of connection to a prehistory stretching back tens of millions of years; it also gave us a sense of hope for the future. Even more exceptional, though more modest in size, is Tasmania's amazing King's Holly, which may have sprouted its first green shoots before modern human beings evolved. This strange, heroic little tree has somehow kept itself alive the whole time, far longer than any other individual plant or animal on the planet.

Trees form the backbone of our natural heritage, with the vast Australian continent home to some 40 billion of them. They come in all shapes and sizes and in thousands of different species, rejoicing in such quirky names as axe-breaker and lilly pilly and zigzag wattle. Without them, life could not have evolved in the unique way it has; three-quarters of our native trees occur naturally only here. In the 60 million years since Australia broke free from the ancient supercontinent of Gondwana, many marvellous oddities have evolved in splendid seclusion.

We would do well to take a humbler view of our own place in Australia's natural scheme of things and to view our native trees more generously. Our relationship with them has always been an uneasy one, more pragmatic than aesthetic. Trees suffer from being useful; we take for granted the many services they provide. Imagine your neighbourhood without trees and all they supply: the shade, cooling, oxygen, windbreaks, privacy, colour, bird-roosts, fruits, flowers and a visual feast of movement in the breeze. How about the power poles to carry your electricity and hold the street lights that chase away the dark? Or the palings and picket fences that define and defend your property boundaries? Or the beams, rafters, joists and bearers that make up the sturdy backbones of your home? Or perhaps the handsome dining table that is the centrepiece of your family and social life?

Muscular axemen in their white singlets, almost surgically dismembering a log in the frantic woodchop events at agricultural shows, remind us how much of our national wealth and strength was built on the life-and-limb sacrifice of trees. Think ringbark, chainsaw, woodchip and dieback: some twenty billion have fallen. The many thousands of Landcare groups, bush regenerators, farmers and graziers now busy replanting native trees by the million across the landscape – to battle oozing salt scalds, to stabilise erosion-scarred hillsides and riverbanks, and to save endangered birds and other animals – remind us how much damage was done in ignorance and greed to 'open up' the land.

We should be more conscious that chainsaws, bulldozers and herbicides have given us a greater life-and-death power over our trees than at any previous time in history. They can do without us; we cannot live without them.

Facing page: Twenty billion trees were felled with axes: modern technology has even more awesome power

Eucalypts

Among our many unique trees, one group are quintessential Aussies: the eucalypts. It's easy to underestimate them. They don't have the pretty symmetry of pines and firs, they don't turn on the dazzling autumn displays of maples and elms, and there's a deceptive uniformity in their foliage or form. While many of the bare-trunked gums can be stunningly beautiful, elegance is not their strong suit. Their leaves are usually a drab green, their bark peels off like sunburnt skin or cracks and flakes like a dried mudpack.

Yet for all that, gum trees have a sturdiness and resilience that seem to encapsulate what it means to live in Australia – that quiet-achiever thing. Despite timeworn soils, heat, lack of water and legions of insect attackers, they manage to survive and stay green year-round. Most miraculous is the eucalypt's ability to be torched by hellish bushfires then spring back to life with a flourish of delicate new growth. Time and again I have walked through bushland after a fire has swept

through and marvelled at the resilience of eucalypt trees, their branches blackened and killed, yet their trunks swathed in fine green pantaloons of new leaf. A few years later, you'd hardly know there'd been a fire: paradoxically, the force of destruction and death is the source of life and renewal for most eucalypts. Their almost casual propensity to burst en masse into flame has made them fire-breathing tyrants threatening other living things.

We may take them for granted because they are so widespread and there are so many, but eucalypts are the backbone of the continent's life-support system. Their nectar and sugary sap are fountains of life for countless birds, bees, bats, bugs and beetles. They are the hotels of the bush as well, teeming throngs of creatures large and small feed and hide on, under or even inside their bark, branches and leaves; their cool dark hollows make safe havens for possums, parrots and even people.

For all their familiarity in the Australian landscape these are exceptional trees, whose ranks include some of the world's tallest and oldest. Eucalypts trace their lineage back perhaps 65 million years, emerging from the wet forests of ancient Australia as the dinosaurs were dying out. Their survival skills are finely honed.

No other type of tree has proved so adaptable, with hundreds of species evolving to conquer many different and difficult habitats across the continent. There's barely an environmental niche anywhere in Australia that doesn't boast a member of this great extended family. Over the ages, eucalypts have done battle with rainforests, giant marsupials the size of cars, ice ages, shifting sea levels and changing climates. Collectively, they carry in their genes the lessons learned from all those contests. Individually, their resilience and capacity to survive for centuries make each one a living record of events during its lifetime: its scars, scorch marks, amputated limbs, hollows and burls tell of storm, fire, flood, drought, disease and adversity. Among the billions of eucalypts that share our continent today are many veterans that began their lives long before the early European explorers sailed into view of the great southern land and first sniffed the scent of eucalyptus on the breeze. Australia's greatest tree? Without a doubt, the not-so-humble old gum.

Going, going . . . .

The Bennelong Twins

SYDNEY, NEW SOUTH WALES

It's the breathtaking view snapped a thousand times a day by tourist cameras, the one that unmistakeably defines just where you are in the world, the one that screams Australia. Soaring improbably into the sky in the foreground are the bleach-white sails of the world's most beautiful and original building, the Sydney Opera House. Sparkling around it are the deep blue waters of the world's finest harbour. In the background is the world's largest and best-known steel arch bridge, the Old Coathanger itself.

Of all the places to drink in this iconic vision of modern Australia, the best vantage point is the level lawn at the northern end of the ridge on Bennelong Point, just above the Opera House. You can reach it via the Tarpeian Way steps, hewn into the sandstone cliff that marks the abrupt end of the ridge. A path at the top leads to a gate in a wrought-iron fence bordering the Domain, the public land set aside from development with great foresight in 1788 by Governor Phillip. You'll pass some wonderful old Port Jackson figs, a legacy of the grand landscaping passions of the late nineteenth century. These massive natives of the harbourside have thrown out great arching broad-leafed canopies that rest on sculpted trunks propped by curtain-folds of buttress roots. Behind you, above the crowns of other large trees, is the romantic crenellated roof line of Government House. The path leads to the Bennelong Lawn, a quiet and intimate perch above the hustle and bustle of tourism, the churning ferries and the ceaseless hum of Australia's greatest city. The magical scene with its stunning backdrop is a favourite of photographers and lovers. This quiet little patch of land with water views would be the quintessential piece of Sydney real estate, worth millions. Happily, it is public land and everyone can enjoy it for free.

Facing page:
The Bennelong Lawn:
nothing alerts visitors
to these special trees

Imagine the extraordinary changes you would have witnessed if you had somehow been able to stand there and watch the unfolding panorama of life below over the past few centuries. You would have observed the original inhabitants of this part of Sydney, the Cadigal people, going about their lives. Their country – Cadi – was the southern side of the harbour, from what is now Darling Harbour east to South Head. This point was known as Toobegully and from here you would have seen the smoke of a thousand campfires and women out fishing in their flimsy canoes. You would have heard the thud of stone axes, the laughter of children and sometimes the ancient songs of the mysterious Kangaroo and Dog Dance initiation ceremony held on the waterside flats of Woccanmagully, now known as Farm Cove.

You would have seen angry Cadigal men brandishing spears and clubs and heard their 'horrid howl' and angry cries of protest as the ships of the First Fleet dropped anchor on 25 January 1788. Throughout that momentous day you would have witnessed the landing of convict work parties, the first tents erected, the British flag unfurled, gun shots fired into the air and toasts drunk to a nation on the other side of the planet. Soon enough, you would have heard metal axes ring as the trees began to come down – sawn up or blown up and dragged off to be burnt, used for lumber or simply dumped into the sea, a practice that would no doubt have horrified the Cadigal. Sydney Cove and Farm Cove were, after all, the points of first contact – perhaps collision is a better word – between European society and

The Bennelong Twins: witnesses to our history

the far more ancient one in which the bush provided for all human needs. This was the beginning of its end in this part of the world.

Suppose you could have watched all that followed over the next two centuries. To your right, the Domain and the Gardens would remain green but the bush would be cleared, farms would come and go, the shoreline would be contained in tidy stone walls, Woccanmagully would be filled and the land surface altered and smoothed beyond recognition. To your left, the new colony would stutter into growth then spread with extraordinary vigour into a great city that now teems and sprawls far into the distance with 4.5 million people. You would have seen Sydney Cove utterly engulfed by a towering world of concrete, glass and steel, the two sides of the harbour bridged by steel, and the amazing Opera House rise beneath your feet.

Virtually unknown and unnoticed, two trees at this special site have lived through all this. Perched on a cliff's edge – literally and metaphorically – an extraordinary pair of forest red gums has somehow managed to survive the transformation of their world. They are elegant twins that grow huddled together where they germinated, probably in the early 1700s, not much more than a metre apart (it is assumed they are two trees but they may, in fact, be Siamese twins with fused root systems, or perhaps even just one tree with dual trunks). They probably began as tiny seeds from the same parent tree, which has long gone.

They are not especially tall, perhaps 25 metres, but their crowns rise above the tips of the Opera House sails. They seem surprisingly healthy. The tree on the left as you face the harbour is the stouter of the two, with a smooth mottled trunk more than a metre in diameter. Typically for gum trees, the trunks are bare of branches for many metres: they both fork early into a few thick branches that ascend sharply to a classic open eucalypt crown, fanned out and layered in clutches of lank, leathery leaves that give see-through glimpses of the sky. Their bark is a smooth skin that sheds in large flakes to create a patchwork of grey, slaty blue and white. In winter, they put on a fair show of fluffy white blossom, bursting in clumps from funny little pale green buds with long pointed caps, like clowns' hats. Bats, birds and bees feed on the rich nectar. Ants take the seeds they drop. They offer dappled shade to two bench seats placed beneath them, where many a weary tourist or city worker has sat to rest and revive amid the litter of narrow brown leaves and little gumnuts.

It is remarkable that these trees still stand and thrive. They are the last of their kind so close to the city, a literal stone's throw from the nation's longest-settled, most crowded and heavily used precinct. I have no hesitation in nominating them as Australia's most important historic trees. Their survival has been against incredible odds.

Where the Opera House now stands, for example, was once a tidal flat leading to a small island. Between 1818 and 1821, the island and shore rocks were levelled and the flat was filled with the rubble. A large square fortress with castellated battlements, Fort Macquarie, was built there with sandstone quarried from the cliff. Various quarrying exercises over the years all stopped just metres from where the two red gums grew (Fort Macquarie was demolished in 1901 for electric tramway sheds, that in turn were replaced by the Sydney Opera House). Sydney Cove, Bennelong Point, the Domain and Farm Cove were gradually cleared of bushes and trees. Cattle and goats grazed nearby. Even when Government House was built just behind them, when the Tarpeian steps were cut from the cliff below them, when a fence was erected beside them, when grand ornamental gardens and parks were planted around them, the Bennelong Twins somehow were spared each time.

Going, going . . .

They also survived the Depression years, when the hundreds of homeless dossers lived rough in the Domain and helped themselves to its trees for firewood and shelter. Nor have termites, diseases, fires, fierce winds, hailstorms or lightning strikes laid them low. As direct living links to the full span of Australia's birth and growth, they are unique and irreplaceable.

In the 1870s, an elderly resident of Sydney wrote a memoir of her long life in the city. Jane Maria Cox (née Brooks) had been born in London to well-off parents, who brought their daughter to the new colony in 1813. Unlike many of the new arrivals, the Brooks family came to Sydney not as convicts or officials but as free settlers in their own ship, which they then sold in a canny exchange for five stores, a country house, a large block of land on the corner of Pitt and Hunter streets and a stone cottage with a garden. In her journal, Cox recalled:

> After getting settled in our Cottage and getting a Pew in St Phillip's, my Father and Mother thought after our studies were over, we should walk; round Benalong's Point . . . was our favourite. It was by the water side, a raised terrace walk under the Government Domain Wall, a seat at the end, then a steep flight of steps to go up to the higher ground. I remember that natives used to sleep there in little Gunyahs made of Bushes, but our Governess did not like to go too near them as the fish they were eating for supper did not smell too well. In our early morning walk we could see very tiny canoes with a Gin fishing in them quite alone, sometimes a streak of smoke from it, and we supposed she was cooking.

With such wonderful history so intrinsic to this site, it is incomprehensible that nothing here alerts the visitor to its significance, and especially its marvellous twin trees. They are dramatically lit at night but there's no sign, no plaque telling of what they are, their age or their cultural value. They are not mentioned in the major visitors' guides. No ceremonies are held in their honour. They do have heritage listing – as part of the Domain – but no special precautions are taken to protect them.

The only specific mention of them that I could find in any official document is in the current master plan for the Domain, which notes: 'To the north of Government House, close to the Tarpeian Way, is a eucalypt(s) which appears to have been photographed in 1858 and 1864 and is identifiable in a c.1901 photograph.' Thankfully, that plan recommends the conservation of this and other remnants of the original native plant cover, in keeping with the activities of the adjoining Royal Botanic Gardens. Seeds have been collected from the twins, in case of calamity. But is that enough?

The First Fleet Survivors

SYDNEY, NEW SOUTH WALES

The Bennelong Twins are certainly not the only remnants of Sydney Harbour's original bushland. From where they stand you can see more complete examples on Bradley's Head just across the harbour, and on other headlands as well. But like the twins, they have survived as much by default as good management, mostly thanks to being reserved for fortifications, quarantine and military facilities. Happily, awareness is growing of the value of these remnants; most are now incorporated into Sydney Harbour National Park, and they should survive many more years for future generations to enjoy. They still have secrets to reveal. As recently as 1986, for example, a new species of diminutive casuarina tree was discovered in remnant bushland on the foreshore of Nielsen Park, a few kilometres down the harbour. Named the Nielsen Park she-oak, it is known only from that site but was probably more widespread in the past. At the time of its discovery, the total population numbered just ten plants – two males and eight females. They were found just in time because they were aged and in decline: the females produced seed for only two more years and by 2003, all ten were dead. Conservation officials were, however, able to avert the tree's extinction by collecting and propagating enough seed to put a recovery program into effect. New saplings of the Nielsen Park she-oak are now growing at the original site and other harbourside locations.

I walked with Doug Benson through the Royal Botanic Gardens, discussing how many early visitors to Sydney Harbour commented on its lush cover of woodlands, shrubs, herbs and grasses; to European eyes, Australia's unusual plants were as befuddling and surprising as its bizarre animals. Some found the evergreen bush drab, missing the bright green flush of the northern spring and the vibrant displays of

Going, going . . .

Doug Benson

Doug Benson, a plant ecologist with the Royal Botanic Gardens, Sydney, is working to ensure that other rare survivors in the Sydney region get their best chance. Benson and colleague Jocelyn Howell have done as much as anyone to document and study Sydney's remnant plant life. Plants have held a lifelong fascination for him, as he explained when he took me on a guided tour of the trees that survive closest to the city in the Domain and Gardens precincts.

'In my family photo album there's a childhood picture of me when I was four or five tugging a little red wagon, its tray laden with potted plants for the garden,' he says. Growing up in suburban inner Sydney, his passion found its first outlet in gardens and parks: there was no proverbial patch of bush at the end of the street for him to play in, because there was no bush left. Perhaps it was that gaping emptiness in the landscape that sparked what was to become a lifetime's work. He has a vivid memory of going with his father to a public garbage dump at Homebush, where from the family car his dad gestured expansively across the scene before them. It was good, his father explained to him, that the mangrove swamp was being filled in. It was progress. One day this would be levelled, covered with soil and grassed to become a wonderful sporting venue with playing fields for kids like him. His father was right about the sporting venue – the 2000 Olympic Games were held there. Benson thinks his dad was wrong, though, about the mangroves: 'Even then I can remember thinking that I didn't want more grass, I wanted the mangrove trees to be kept.'

As an adult he was able to combine his interests in botany and history and, with Howell, he has systematically identified and mapped the city's original plant cover and what remains of it.

autumn colour. Others came to appreciate more subtle shades of green, the absence of depressing skeletal winter trees and the different spring delights of creamy flannel flowers and spectacular crimson waratahs.

Arriving with the First Fleet, Watkin Tench showed in his journal observations of Sydney Harbour that he, for one, liked the look of the place:

> The general face of the country is certainly pleasing, being diversified with gentle ascents, and winding little vallies, covered for the most part with large spreading trees, which afford a succession of leaves in all seasons. In those places where trees are scarce, a variety of lowering shrubs abound, most of them entirely new to a European, and surpassing in beauty, fragrance, and number, all I ever saw in an uncultivated state: among these, a tall shrub, bearing an elegant white flower, which smells like English May, is particularly delightful.

Benson says the shrub was most likely a tea-tree or a paperbark, both of which can put on cloud-like displays of blossom and a warm scent that encourages you to open your lungs and inhale your fill. The native trees certainly got attention. The surgeon aboard the *Lady Penrhyn*, Arthur Bowes Smyth, enthused in his journal on 26 January 1788 that 'distinct plantations of the tallest and most stately trees I ever saw in any nobleman's ground in England, can not excel in beauty those wh[ich] Nature now presented to our view'.

But the trees stood in the way of the settlers' ambitions. The first landing party at Sydney Cove, led by Governor Arthur Phillip, set straight away to a task that they and successive generations were to carry out with extraordinary vigour and grim efficiency for the next two centuries – cutting down trees:

> The governor, with a party of marines, and some artificers selected from amongst the seamen of the *Sirius* and the convicts, arrived in Port Jackson, and anchored off the mouth of the cove intended for the settlement on the evening of the 25th; and in the course of the following day sufficient ground was cleared for encamping the officer's guard and the convicts who had been landed in the morning. The spot chosen for this purpose was at the head of the cove, near the run of fresh water, which stole silently along through a very thick wood, the stillness of which had then, for the first time since the creation, been interrupted by the rude sound of the labourer's axe, and the downfall of its ancient inhabitants.

What began as a necessity went on to became a national fixation. A few months into 1788, Surgeon Wogan described how the new Australians were occupied: '. . . the principal business has been the clearing of Land, cutting, Grubbing and burning down Trees, sawing up Timber and Plank for Building . . .'

Benson's recreations of the woodlands suggest that scribbly gums, lilly pilly, cheese tree and blueberry ash would have grown by the Tank Stream, along with the forest red gums. 'On the sandstone gullies probably would have been blackbutt, red bloodwood, Sydney peppermint gum and the smooth-barked angophora,' he says. On the small alluvial flat opening onto the harbour, now filled and covered by Circular Quay, swamp oaks and probably swamp mahogany would have grown, with Port Jackson figs nestled into the surrounding rocky outcrops.

The gum trees had their detractors but they held more than a few hidden aces. Naval officer Henry Waterhouse later wrote:

> It will be necessary to observe, that there is so much resinous gum in the Wood, that it appears to be impervious to Water – for many Logs, on the first forming of the Settlement in 1788, were cut down, and rolled into the Water (Salt) to clear the Land – which Logs, when taken up again in 1798, were as sound as when cut down – not the smallest appearance of decay ... I am therefore induced to think the Wood of New South Wales more durable than Oak or Teak ... Where this wood has been used for planking a Ship, it has been found of so hard a nature, that a Scraper would hardly touch it – and a Nail; drove in, the Carpenter of the *Reliance* said they could not get it out again.

Even so, a pervasive idea seems to have taken hold among the early settlers – encouraged by subsidies that rewarded land-clearing – that they were in a kind of protracted contest against the trees and the bush, which needed to be bludgeoned into submission and transformed into something more recognizable to European eyes.

Soon the removal of trees around the colony was effected so well that environmental problems were apparent. Governor King, for example, was forced in 1803 to issue a General Order against the removal of trees from riverbanks in an effort to prevent erosion.

By 1812, William Hutchinson, the Principal Superintendent of Convicts, described the Domain as 'little better than a rocky waste full of large stumps'. The city area was largely denuded of native plants by the 1830s, Benson says. Most settlers gave little care or protection even to trees significant to themselves. The *Sydney Herald* ran the following paragraph on 7 May 1832: 'A swamp oak at the lower end of George Street, near the Dock-yard, upon which the British Flag was first hoisted in this town, has been lately cut down by the gang employed in repairing the streets. The tree was considered sacred by Governor Macquarie and old hands of the colony.'

It wasn't just that trees stood in the way of progress; they were not valued in their own right. As Louisa Meredith complained in 1839:

> The system of 'clearing' here, by the total destruction of every native tree and shrub, gives a more bare, raw and ugly appearance to a new place. In England, we plant groves and woods, and think our country residences unfinished and incomplete without them; but here the exact contrary is the case, and unless a settler can see an expanse of bare, naked, unvaried, shadeless, dry, dusty land spread all around him, he fancies his dwelling 'wild and uncivilised'.

The old blackbutt that keeps watch over the Domain

The Domain still featured quite a few large native trees – mainly eucalypts such as blackbutt, Sydney peppermint gum, red mahogany, scribbly gum, red bloodwood and angophoras – until about 1860, although barely a twig of understorey remained. Left stranded, lacking fresh recruits or human encouragement, most of the old trees started dying off around 1870, as Benson points out. The result today is that the Bennelong Twins are part of a select but dwindling band of less than twenty individual trees in the Domain and Gardens that date back to pre-European times. One of them stands right outside the entrance to the offices where Benson and Howell work. A large blackbutt keeps watch over the roadway that carries countless visitors along the Domain ridgetop to the famous Mrs Macquarie's Chair, but few would realise its significance. Mrs Macquarie herself would have seen this tree in her time and it was she who planned

the route to skirt past it. As we paid our respects to this remarkable old sentry, a raucous white cockatoo swooped in to land in its branches: it cocked its head, eyed us off, raised its lairy sulphur crest then belted out its trademark throat-clearing screech. It seemed fair comment.

Within the Gardens themselves there are five forest red gums thought to date back to 1788. We soon reached the largest and probably the oldest: its trunk is a respectable 3.1 metres in girth. It is the only one of all the First Fleet veterans to carry a sign noting its age and provenance. It is, however, quite dead. Branches that once reached up to twenty metres high have been cut back for public safety. Benson noted sadly that it had expired only months earlier. There was no announcement at the time: after perhaps three or four centuries this great Sydney veteran passed on without fanfare or any public attention at all. Its grey trunk is being conserved in situ as an animal habitat; birds, bats and possums thrive here, but its main occupant is a hive of feral non-native honeybees that have taken over one of its ancient hollows. Another veteran forest red gum can be seen alive

A very special tree

To keep or remove a tree? This is a dilemma our Arborist team faces every day.

This 'unattractive' Forest Red Gum (*Eucalyptus tereticornis*) is being spared the chop because it holds great historical and cultural significance and is not considered to be a threat to public safety at this stage.

We are keeping it because:

• It is native to this site and believed to be one of the oldest trees here.

• It is home to native bees, possums, cicadas and other wildlife.

• Our Education staff and the Indigenous community refer to it as a 'supermarket tree' because eucalypts have so many uses – honey for drinking, bark for wrapping, resident animals for eating, wood for canoes and tools.

John Len
students

nearby, beside the fence south of the Henry Lawson Gate. Some 15 metres tall and with a girth of 2.5 metres, it is a wonderfully charismatic old tree with a quirky spiralling bark that looks as if someone has twisted it like soft toffee. It's a much-admired tree and a favourite perch for birds.

Just north-west of the Maiden Pavilion the meandering path down to Farm Cove takes a gentle dive. 'This is where the old shoreline of the cove probably was before it was filled for the Lower Gardens,' says Benson, gesturing across to a bank that runs in an obvious contour across the slope. It's hard now to conjure up the sights and sounds of the Kangaroo and Dog Dance. But my imagination spins when Benson alerts me to the fine tall swamp oaks that grace this slope. Three adults of these soft and elegant casuarina trees are clustered near each other; they top 15 metres in height and one has a girth of over two metres. Judging by their size, age and position, Benson believes these special trees used to grow on the water's edge, their usual preferred position. The fact that they are growing so close together suggests that they are suckers, or clones, and thus the living shoots of an even more ancient stem.

Close by are more signs of the lost shoreline, a group of three large Port Jackson figs that command the rocky sandstone outcrops west of Victoria

Lodge. These figs are long-lived denizens of Sydney Harbour, but their age is hard to estimate because they thicken their trunks fitfully according to seasonal conditions, not to an annual growth cycle that produces tree rings that enable accurate dating. Many Port Jackson figs were planted in and around Sydney in colonial times – along with the more statuesque Moreton Bay figs native to the Illawarra region – and some are now of considerable size and stature. But only four others in this area are thought to be pre-European originals. All of them cling to the steep cliff face of Bennelong Point, their plump roots looking like molten candlewax as they slither down the rockface and probe its crevices for nutrients and water. Like the Bennelong twins that tower directly above them, they create a unique 'sense of place', as Benson puts it, that connects us directly to the birth and growth of modern Australia. The fact that they are largely unknown and ignored suggests that we still haven't shaken off the colonial mindset. For the most part, native trees are no longer seen as enemies, but we don't yet accord them their rightful and respected place in our own family 'tree'.

The Macarthur Olive

ROSEHILL, NEW SOUTH WALES

John Macarthur was obstreperous, quarrelsome and, quite frankly, more and more bonkers as he grew older. Yet he was one of the outstanding figures of the early colony of New South Wales, well known for his prominent role in Australia's only armed takeover of government, the 1808 Rum Rebellion. For all his faults, the relentless energy and foresight Macarthur put into promoting grazing and agriculture has left an enduring legacy. He may be best known for his role in developing the wool industry but his interests were extraordinarily wide, as old records reveal from his properties at Rosehill and Camden, outside Sydney. The beautiful houses built there by him and his wife Elizabeth – an exceptional person in her own right – remain to this day.

Elizabeth Farm at Rosehill began its life in 1793 as a simple unadorned country cottage with an ornamental garden of exotic trees, shrubs, bulbs and annual flowers. The Macarthurs quickly established a busy and prosperous farm and were virtually self-sufficient by 1794, when the property's livestock included 130 goats, 100 hogs, two cows and many kinds of poultry. They could also call on produce from a vineyard, a vegetable garden and a fruit orchard, not to mention many cultivated paddocks of wheat, corn and potatoes. The abundant local wildlife brought even more food to the table. John Macarthur wrote in 1794:

Facing page: Australia's oldest surviving exotic tree, an olive planted in 1805

I have received no stock from Government, but one Cow, the rest I have either purchased or bred. With the assistance of One Man & Half a dozen greyhounds which I keep, my Table is constantly supplied with Wild Ducks or Kangaroos averaging one week with another, these Dogs do not kill less than three hundred pounds weight…

If Trees Could Speak

Still sprouting and bearing fruit, but showing its age

As their wealth grew, they created a classic colonial home around the cottage. It had wide verandas, French doors, marble fireplaces and lavish use of cedar joinery. Some of the original parts of the old cottage are still intact within the house and are the oldest surviving residential buildings of their type in Australia. Although the farmland is long gone, the Historic Houses Trust of New South Wales maintains the house in excellent condition and it attracts many visitors each year.

Back in 1805, John Macarthur arrived home in Australia after a four-year absence. He had been sent to England to face a court martial but cannily had the charges dropped and resigned from the army. Instead of returning in disgrace, he was now an ambitious trader, armed with letters of support from Lord Camden and a promise of large tracts of land in a location of his own choice. Elizabeth, no slouch herself, had run the farm while he was gone, organising a workforce that included 24 convicts, and had doubled its flock to more than 4000 sheep. The cargo her husband brought back with him is best remembered for another kind of sheep: the small flock of Spanish merinos that he had artfully liberated from the Royal Flock and that were to help make vast fortunes in years to come.

Far less well known is that Macarthur also brought a huge variety of plants on the same ship. Scores of different kinds of ornamental flowers and shrubs, oak trees, grape vines and an extraordinary array of fruit trees he intended to trial under Australian conditions. Some thrived and others wilted in the heat. But one that took to its new circumstances like a duck to water was an olive tree. Within weeks of its arrival the Macarthurs had it planted just a few metres from their house, and away it went. Perhaps the tree got such a privileged position because it had special significance for them. In a letter to the Colonial Office in 1805, Macarthur wrote: 'Amongst the plants that I have been so fortunate as to bring out alive is the olive, and I hope as an emblem of Peace its branches, and that blessing, will spread together and be universally propagated throughout the whole country.'

For now, however, the olive had to vie for attention with a veritable horn of plenty: among other things the farm was soon producing oranges, lemons, almonds, grapes, peaches, apricots, nectarines, medlars, raspberries, apples, pears, strawberries, walnuts, cherries, plums, loquats, citrons, shaddocks, cherries, guavas, pomegranates, figs, melons, gooseberries, currants, mulberries and capers.

Even so, historical records show that the Macarthurs' experimental cultivation of olives at their two farms continued for several decades and included bottling samples of olive oil to send to family contacts in England in search of business opportunities. Visiting the property later, in 1831, Major Thomas Mitchell marvelled at the health and vigour of many of these shrubs and trees, including the olive.

Today, all of them are gone – except the olive. We can't be absolutely certain that it's the same tree, but it is the oldest on the property and in the opinion of professional arborists, has all the hallmarks of a 200-year-old veteran. No other foreign tree planted in the early days of the colony has survived so long. It's an unprepossessing tree, with a wizened and fluted stump of a trunk from which it manages to produce plenty of vigorous new shoots. One of its largest stems had to be removed some years back after termites got into it, and a hole in its deadwood has been filled with unattractive expanding foam, but it's showing no sign of flagging. It even manages to produce fruit occasionally, smallish black olives that are a bit shrivelled and bitter. When there was concern for its wellbeing during a drought a few years ago, the Historic Houses Trust decided to make 250 cuttings of it to spread around the country to ensure the tree lived on, but only a few of them struck. Since then the Elizabeth Farm gardener has had better success.

It would be nice to think that this great old olive – Australia's oldest surviving exotic tree – carries on for many years more: not only for the small supporting role it played in the building of the nation but to continue the hope expressed by John Macarthur, that it would be 'an emblem of Peace'.

Trees with spirit

The Seven Peacekeepers

SYDNEY REGION, NEW SOUTH WALES

Indigenous Australians have an ancient human relationship to celebrate with trees, an intimate one that recognises human dependency on them. We don't exactly know when or how the first people came but it was long, long ago and they came by sea. They may have been adventurous *Homo erectus* people as far back as a million years ago, or the more modern humans who first ventured here from Indonesia tens of thousands of years ago. Either way, the absence of a land bridge during that time means they must have sailed on water craft made of wood. Trees thus played as much of a foundation role in the first human occupation of the land as they did for the more recent European settlers. And, no doubt, Australia's strange and wonderful trees must have been every bit as unfamiliar to both groups of people at first.

To those first Australians, trees would have been bountiful and prized sources of food, fuel, raw materials, shelter and shade, as they were for all who followed. They yielded boomerangs, didgeridoos, woomeras, spears, fighting shields, coolamons and burial posts. They stored precious water resources in arid lands. They were the supermarket, the hardware store, the pharmacy and the corner shop. Their seasonal changes were watched closely for signs that certain food resources were available or that cultural events were nigh. Trees were, as well, a source of Aboriginal lore and law, home to or representative of watchful spirit figures, demons and heroes.

The association of certain species with each other, for example, took on a deeper significance than the merely botanical, and instructive stories were woven around them. In *Gum: the Story of Eucalypts and their Champions*, author Ashley Hay relates the tale of the seven peacekeepers, as told by the D'harawal people who occupied the coastal strip of New South Wales south of Botany Bay.

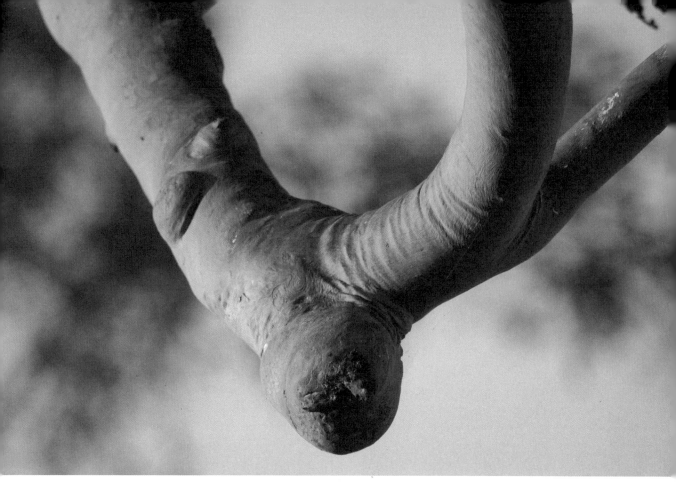

A leader named Yandel'bana had enlisted seven warriors to establish peace between the clans of their country, but was being thwarted by malevolent Wiree spirits. A plot was hatched to lure the Wiree into a trap. The seven warriors disguised themselves as species of eucalypt trees. One who knew medicines was transformed into a gum whose leaves yielded a vapour to treat illness. Another, known as a firemaker, became a gum whose fibrous bark was used as tinder. Others took on disguises of gums that yielded specific weapons, or were used to smoke out evil spirits or to provide shelter.

The seven trees formed themselves into a circle and Yandel'bana took pieces from each of them – bark, leaves, branches, gumnuts, nectar and roots – to build a campfire in its centre. Yandel'bana pretended to sleep by the fire as it threw showers of sparks into the night sky, to fill it with stars. This beacon drew in the Wiree, who saw the lone man sleeping and resolved to steal his spirit. They entered his camp in disguise, using his mother's voice to stir him from sleep. Then the trap was sprung and the seven warriors shook off their leaves and bark, joined hands and closed in. The Wiree tried to escape by transforming into a chaotic whirlwind, or willy-willy, but the warriors prevailed and fire consumed the evil spirits. When the dust settled, each warrior had sustained a single wound. One had lost a tooth, one some skin from his leg and one had a bloody arm. One had a bald patch of missing hair, another had wet, swollen eyes; one who lost a branch in the fire was now missing a little finger and the one who gave a root to Yandel'bana was missing a toe.

After living out their lives in that country, the seven warriors died and once more became the type of tree they had been that fateful night. Their names became those of the relevant species: Mai'andowi, a smooth-barked gum; Bai'yali, a stringy-bark; Boo'angi, a spotted gum; Terri'yergro, a scaly-barked gum; Kai'yerro, a ribbon gum; Bourrounj, a peppermint gum; and Mugga'go, an ironbark [mugga ironbark is the common name today for *Eucalyptus sideroxylon*]. As for Yandel'bana, he became an angophora, the eye-catching tree with the smoothly rounded pink body and improbably angular limbs that dwells among the gums.

The Canoe Tree

MELBOURNE, VICTORIA

At this quiet place in Yarra Park, there's no doubting you're in Melbourne: the towering outer walls of the Melbourne Cricket Ground are so close that a burly batsman could probably reach them from here with a well-struck ball. Yet few who visit Australia's hallowed temple of sport would realise that two of Australia's great trees stand nearby. Indeed, on a casual stroll through the park you could walk straight past and barely notice them. The plaza outside the MCG's nearby Olympic Stand boasts larger-than-life statues commemorating the history-making achievements of sporting greats Don Bradman and Betty Cuthbert. But these two trees are graced only with a modest plaque and a low, rusty fence.

They are not spectacular to look at. Yet they deserve attention because they, too, have a history-making tale of achievement to tell. That may seem an odd claim to make about a couple of grey, dead and decaying old tree stumps. But their significance stems from where they are and what they represent, not how they look today.

Take a closer look: come and sit near the larger of the two stumps and take in the scene. It's a sunny day, with a light breeze blowing and a smattering of clouds. Someone is walking a dog in the distance and we can hear occasional birdsong. We are amid rolling green parkland, the expansive lawns, handsome gum trees and casuarinas. A wide sealed pathway runs right next to the tree and some unsympathetic soul has erected a tall modern lamppost almost adjacent to it. Looking south, the MCG is to our right and the famous Punt Road ground of the Richmond Football Club is farther away to the left. Down the hill you can hear a background hum of traffic on Brunton Avenue, running parallel to the milk-chocolate waters of the Yarra River, sliding along at the base of the slope a few hundred metres away.

We are looking at the remains of an ancient river red gum. It is a very large stump, a couple of metres across at ground level, and must have been a fine tree in its prime. Its characterful trunk rises a good eight metres or so before ending at a fork where several large branches have been sawn off. The rotting stubs of other large limbs, grown and dropped, attest to its life history and its substantial age. The main bole still bears streaks of colour, suggesting it has not been all that long since the juices of life flowed just beneath its bark. On its southern side, away from the sun, moss and lichen grow on its base, which has lightly buttressed roots to steady its grip. If you had to liken its appearance to something, it's pretty much like a giant elephant's leg, complete with chubby toes. If that suggests an alien feel to this tree, it is because of all that has happened here to change its surroundings so dramatically. Make no mistake, this tree most definitely belongs here and nowhere else.

What makes it a unique conduit to the past is to be seen on the north side. There, a deep and mighty scar is obvious, a patch of long-dead wood stretching almost the full width of the tree and reaching up three metres or more. This massive slice of its skin was removed when it was still alive, but the wound didn't kill the tree; it continued to grow for some considerable time afterwards, as is obvious by the thick curved lip of new wood that has folded around the edges of the scar.

If you close your eyes, ignore the traffic sounds and focus on the wattlebird's grating cough and the peewits jeering loudly from the nearby treetops, you may be able to transport yourself back in time to when this scar was made. Imagine it is 1834, the year before John Batman sailed up the Yarra in the sloop *Rebecca*, the first white man to enter this world. It is early morning and the low-angled sunlight gives the great red gum a soft golden glow. Insects buzz in its flowers and a wedge-tailed eagle perches high up in the crown, lord of a wooded hillside running down to a wetland and a Yarra that runs clear and clean and is alive with ducks and fish. To the right, instead of the MCG, there's an expanse of open ground mainly covered in dense swards of kangaroo grass. The peewits are still there, but this time they are calling in alarm because three dark-skinned men have trekked through the grass, halted at the base of this tree and are in animated discussion. They are muscular and lean, dark-haired and bearded: one is wearing a beautiful possum-skin cape. One man carries a looped length of stout cord, another holds a staff with a sharpened tip and a third is hefting a stone-headed axe. They circle the tree, pat its trunk solidly with the flats of their hands and point here and there as they examine its bark and inspect it for knots. The eagle cocks its head and peers down at them, holding its perch until one of the men lifts a stone axe and sinks it deep into the trunk with a thud that sets the tree ringing like a tuning fork. The peewits screech in alarm and the eagle lofts itself into the breeze as the axe falls again and again. Sitting on the shoulders of his colleague, the axeman notches higher still until the shape is clear: two parallel lines of notches run vertically up the trunk, tapering to a rounded peak three metres off the ground. The axe is then reversed and all the bark within this outline is given a firm tapping. Then the man with the staff starts working his way methodically around the edges, gently prising and lifting the bark away from the trunk, while the man with the cloak taps in small wooden wedges beneath it. As the slab of bark begins to loosen and come away, the cord is bound around the trunk to hold it in place and prevent its weight from tearing it. Within 30 minutes, the team has carefully levered off the great slab in one piece, loosened the cord and gently lowered it to the ground. They lay their prize on the ground and inspect it with satisfaction, then squat on their haunches for a breather.

Aborigines across Australia had many different uses for many kinds of bark. It served as everything from the roofs and walls of huts and shelters to twine, containers, baby-carriers, kindling, belts and bandages. A piece as large as the one taken from this tree was destined for fashioning into a canoe – an easy form of transport along the nearby Yarra. Aboriginal water craft took many forms: there were wooden and reed rafts, dugout canoes, tied and sewn canoes made from a single sheet of bark and even flat bark canoes for calm river and lake sailing. They sometimes featured a dried mud or flat stone hearth, where a low fire could be kept smouldering for warmth, cooking or to deter insects. Because they usually could be made so quickly and easily, it was a convenient and expedient way to move people and supplies about in rivers and wetlands and to gain access to a wider range of resources.

In this part of the country a big river red gum was often chosen, especially the bark of the lower trunk to take advantage of its natural curvature. The bark was cut by preference after heavy rain, when it was sappy and easier to remove intact, or in the early morning. While it was still pliable, this slab was usually suspended for a short time over a low fire to cure it and enhance its natural curl. It was braced with wooden spreaders, bound tightly with twine and vines at the bow and stern and sealed with a dense plug of clay mixed with twigs, leaves and resin. The scars are often pointed at one end and broad at the other, indicating the bow and stern of the canoe respectively. The recent film *Ten Canoes* has revived interest in this ancient craft.

Trees with spirit

It was a simple but effective form of everyday water transport and far less time-consuming than shaping a more robust canoe for more testing waters. The size of the resultant scar on the tree roughly indicates the size of the canoe made from it: a 1.5-metre strip may have been for a child's canoe, while a four-metre strip may have yielded a vessel capable of carrying several people. One scarred tree in the Barmah Forest area reportedly carries an eight-metre scar, the making of which must have required scaffolds to support the axemen working at such a height. One nineteenth-century European observer described the process:

A few notches were cut with the tomahawk, one above the other, in its bark just outside of what was to be its edge, or gunwale of the canoe. The operator having then roughly marked out on the tree the lines of his vessel, commenced cutting the bark along them with his tomahawk down to the wood, so as to detach from the tree an unbroken sheet of bark, which would be the canoe. To effect this the tree was ascended gradually, by placing the big toe in the notches before mentioned, which were used as steps, the Blackfellow holding on with one hand, whilst he plied the tomahawk with the other hand. He also, I remember, assisted himself by rearing against the tree a stout branch which happened to be at hand, and using it as a ladder to stand on whilst he chopped.

Simple though they were to make, much skill and dexterity was required to sail them safely. Many early records describe with an equal mix of incredulity and admiration how this was accomplished. Watkin Tench, a keen observer of the process in the early days of the colony at Sydney Harbour, described how a couple would wake at first light and go to the water with a burning firebrand in hand to commence their daily fishing excursions. The division of labour meant that women did most of the waterborne fishing.

In general, the canoe is assigned to her, into which she puts the fire and pushes off into deep water, to fish with hook and line. If she have a child at the breast, she takes it with her. And thus in her skiff, a piece of bark tied at both ends with vines, and the edge of it just above the surface of the water, she pushes out regardless of the elements, if they be but commonly agitated.

To the dismay of European observers the infant would ride on her shoulders, grasping her hair, but Tench notes that accidents were few and that the need for the mother to control the stability of her craft probably explained this successful arrangement.

> The management of the canoe alone appears a work of insurmountable difficulty, its breadth is so inadequate to its length. The Indians [Aborigines], aware of its ticklish formation, practice from infancy to move in it without risk. Use only could reconcile them to the painful position in which they sit in it: they drop in the middle of the canoe upon their knees, and resting the buttocks on the heels, extend the knees to the sides, against which they press strongly, so as to form a poise, sufficient to retain the body in its situation, and relieve the weight which would otherwise form wholly upon the toes. Either in this position, or cautiously moving in the centre of the vessel, the mother tends her child; paddles her boat; broils fish; and provides in part the substance of the day.

We'll never know when the MCG tree had its bark removed. But it cannot have been long before John Batman came and saw 'land of the best description, equal to any in the world … the most beautiful sheep pasturage I ever saw in my life'. On 6 June 1835, Batman recorded in his journal that he had signed a 'treaty' with eight 'chiefs' of the local Wurundjeri people, which he claimed was a contract to purchase some 2000 square kilometres of land around Melbourne and another 400 square kilometres around Geelong, to the south-west. The chiefs made their marks on the document and received in exchange 20 pairs of blankets, 30 knives, 12 tomahawks, 12 pairs of scissors, 10 looking glasses, 50 pounds of flour, 50 handkerchiefs, four flannel jackets, four suits of clothes and 12 red shirts. Never mind that the Wurundjeri did not subscribe to the notion of land ownership – rather, they belonged to the land – nor that under British law this was Crown land that they had no legal right to sell. It's even been suggested that there may not have been a treaty at all, that the marks on Batman's contract bore a similarity to markings made on trees in the Parramatta region, near Sydney, where Batman had lived in his youth. Whatever the truth of the matter, other settlers soon followed and the world of the Wurundjeri had changed forever. Their ancient way of life was soon to be in tatters.

Trees with spirit

Part of that way of life involved ceremonial gatherings for social reasons, for law-making, the settlement of disputes and so on. Dancing, singing and feats of physical prowess were part of these events. The land to the west of the scarred tree in Yarra Park was one such place, both camping and corroboree ground. Does that ancient spirit pervade the MCG today and add to its special atmosphere?

In any case, by 1856, the Wurundjeri were all but gone from the area and Governor La Trobe had reserved it as parkland. At one time it also served as a paddock for police horses. Today, there is virtually no trace of Wurundjeri presence in what was once an important, fertile, ancestral place for them. A modern city of almost 3.5 million people has changed their beloved country beyond recognition.

Melbourne also has several notable 'corroboree trees', particularly one in Richmond Park and another in Albert Park. The latter was once a series of swamps and lagoons, but since European settlement it has served variously for grazing stock, as a garbage tip, a camp for the armed services and now extensively for sport (including chariot racing and motor racing) and public recreation. The Corroboree Tree – near Junction Oval, on the corner of Fitzroy Street and Queens Road, St Kilda – is a large river red gum thought to be more than 300 years old. It is the oldest known remnant tree in the Port Phillip area. In mid-2005, a $50 000 project was completed around the Corroboree Tree to control weeds, plant new native grasses and trees and incorporate Aboriginal artwork, in celebration of Aboriginal local history and the contributions of Aborigines to Australian Rules Football. Some of the new plantings of river red gums were from seed propagated from the Corroboree Tree.

Many other significant trees record Aboriginal cultures. Hundreds of carved trees have been listed across south-eastern Australia, often marking places of great cultural significance, such as grave sites and initiation grounds. One initiation place at Binnaway, on the Barwon River, was said to feature up to 80 carved trees. Concentric diamond and triangle motifs featured most conspicuously on south-eastern tree carvings, depicting animal totems, the sun and moon and phenomena such as lightning. Some of these trees were seen as pathways used by sky-heroes to reach the earth during sacred ceremonies. Some still stand in situ, while museums in Melbourne, Sydney and Adelaide hold others. Due to their sacred nature, some may never go on public display. Many others have been consumed by fire, termites and the ravages of time.

One unusual site near Molong in New South Wales marries both Aboriginal and European burial customs at the grave of an exceptional Wiradjuri man named Yuranigh, who was one of three Aboriginal men who accompanied Sir Thomas Mitchell's fourth expedition in 1845 to explore the interior of the continent. It's hard to imagine how the expedition would have fared without Yuranigh, who won the highest praise from

Mitchell for his knowledge of the land, keen judgment and diplomatic skills with the Aboriginal people they encountered. The explorer wrote in his journal that Yuranigh was 'my guide, companion, counsellor and friend on the most eventful occasions during this journey of discovery. His intelligence and judgment rendered him so necessary to me that he was ever at my elbow whether on foot or on horseback. Confidence in him was never misplaced. He knew well the character of all the white men of the party. Nothing escaped his penetrating eye and quick ear'. When he died in 1850, Yuranigh was buried – near Gamboola homestead, about three kilometres south-east of Molong – according to tribal custom. His burial plot was dug between a group of living trees carved with deeply incised geometric designs, featuring diamond and S-shapes and an elongated spiral. The nature of the cuts suggests they were made with a metal axe.

Often an oval or rectangular section of bark was removed and the design was cut into the sapwood beneath, usually facing the burial plot and signifying the dead person's kin and tribal relationships. According to the New South Wales National Parks and Wildlife Service, such carved trees were once widespread in New South Wales but losses due to land clearing, fire and natural deterioration have meant that only about twenty living carved trees are left. Three of the trees around Yuranigh's grave remain alive, and the carved designs can be clearly seen on the tree that has died.

When he learned of Yuranigh's death, Mitchell asked for a headstone and a fence to be erected on the grave as well. When the headstone needed replacing in 1900, a new one was erected at public expense on a Molong marble base, bearing the original stone with its dedication:

> To native courage, honesty and fidelity, Yuranigh, who accompanied the expedition of discovery into tropical Australia in 1846 lies buried here according to the rites of his countrymen and this spot was dedicated and enclosed by the Governor General's Authority in 1852.

Yuranigh's grave is a rare example of two starkly contrasting cultures coexisting in harmony. Its conservation has also been enhanced by the fresh interest shown in it by succeeding generations of citizens and officialdom. In the early 1950s, for example, the owner of the land, W.R. Glasson, put a new a fence around the grave and later donated the land to his local council to manage. Glasson also publicised the site and wrote a paper about Yuranigh for the Royal Geographic Society of Australasia. In 1996, the local Aboriginal Land Council asked for the remains of an unknown Aboriginal person from the Orange area, whose bones had been returned from a museum in Melbourne, to be buried nearby as well.

Trees with spirit

Yuranigh's grave is also a rare example of a historic tree site that has been well cared for and which now has its own formal management plan (adopted in 1999) that treats it in context with its surrounding area – that all-important sense of place. In 1976, following the advice of a tree surgeon, the living trees were treated for insect pests, bark regrowth on two of the trees was removed and the re-exposed carvings were treated with oil. The dead tree is partly sheltered from the elements. The management plan requires weeds to be controlled, fencing to exclude livestock from the site, regeneration of native flora to be actively fostered in a surrounding 1.2 hectare reserve, and the condition of the trees to be regularly monitored. It also encourages better public access and Aboriginal involvement in its management, and calls for interpretive signage to be placed at the site.

Although the carved trees at Yuranigh's grave and the scarred canoe trees at Yarra Park are very different entities, both are irreplaceable records of a shared human history. To me, the Yarra Park trees are particularly special because they have somehow endured in the heart of a massive city. Their contrast with the built world around them is poignant, a sharp reminder of another way of living so much more lightly on the land.

The Yarra River of the Wurundjeri was not the infamously muddy waterway of today but a river so clear and clean that dolphins sometimes swam up it as far as Richmond, according to records cited by the Victorian branch of the National Trust of Australia. The Yarra yielded fish, mussels, eels and waterbirds. Paperbarks on its banks provided soft water-repellent bark for cradling babies. Yams and lily roots were roasted for food. Rushes were used to weave string, mats and baskets. Wattles yielded medicines and a sealant for water containers. Tea-trees, wattles and river red gums were the source of tools and weapons.

The Wurundjeri were part of the Woiworung tribe, which in turn was one of four tribes within the Kulin language group, a nation embracing the Melbourne region and the Yarra catchment, extending right up into the Dandenong Ranges. Remarkably, at the time of European settlement, the whole Woiworung tribe numbered a mere 124 people, says the National Trust. They were organised in bands made up of extended families. Their low numbers, their lifestyle and their capacity to live sustainably in this environment could not contrast more utterly with that of the society that pushed them aside.

James Wandin, a Wurundjeri elder, pointed out to the Victorian Legislative Assembly in an address given on 31 May 2000:

Our people were a hunting-and-gathering people who moved from their camp sites in response to the seasonal availability of resources. Wetlands of the lower Yarra River known as the Birrarung were a rich source of water birds, fish and plant foods, particularly in the summer.

Dispossession of our people also went hand in hand with major destruction of their cultural setting. Forested areas to the north of Melbourne were cleared extensively last century to supply timber for Melbourne and to allow for the establishment of agricultural fields. Trees were cleared; swamps were drained; creek channels were altered; and the habitats for most of their traditional resources were destroyed. The complex mosaic of resource zones that had been used by hundreds of generations of Wurundjeri were replaced by an ever-expanding maze of cobblestone streets lined with factories, shops and houses.

Among the trees and along many creek banks now subsumed by Melbourne was a complex array of camp sites, resource extraction sites, ceremonial sites, sacred sites and a wide range of other places imbued with deep spiritual meaning to the Wurundjeri. Many of these sites are known: ceremonial corroboree grounds once existed at Parliament Hill and close to Merri Creek near Pentridge Jail, and a camp site once existed at the site of the famous Melbourne Cricket Ground.

So Yarra Park is a place of powerful memories, one to respect and treasure. Something I saw on my last visit to the site, when I looked a little more closely at the second scarred tree stump, made it even more remarkable for me. It too is fenced and bears a small obscure plaque, with a footnote that reads: 'Please respect this site. It is

Trees with spirit

important to the Wurundjeri people as traditional custodians of the land and is part of the heritage of all Australians.' This broad stump is only a couple of metres high, a grey relic eaten away by time and termites, with no obvious remaining sign of a scar. I was disappointed to see it partly obscured by tall weeds and looking neglected. Then I looked closer and had to blink to make sure I was seeing right: there, striking out from its decaying flank, was a fresh green shoot of gum leaves. Incredibly, this tree somehow was still alive and striving for the sun. Whatever else it is, for me this ugly, beheaded and weatherbeaten relic is emblematic of the incredible enduring life-force that all trees carry within them.

Facing page: Early settlers were amazed at the tree-climbing skills of Aborigines

Trees with spirit

The Dooligah and Kuritja

MOUNT ANNAN, NEW SOUTH WALES

Aborigines at times marked and decorated significant trees that denoted an important place or had special associations with cultural ceremonies. After the tragic collapse of the local D'harawal society, fourteen such trees carved with designs were found in the Mount Annan area, south-west of Sydney. The trees are no longer there, having been cut down and taken for safekeeping to the Australian Museum. Mysteriously, some of these designs were not linked to D'harawal culture at all, but were peculiar to other tribes and social groups across a large tract of south-eastern Australia. These special trees attest to the fact that Mount Annan was a significant cultural place where the D'harawal played host to visitors from great distances. Contemporary records suggest this was a unique site where people came together every few years for purposes of law-making, marriage and dispute settlement – sort of a parliament, registry office and court combined. The site was known as Yandel'ora.

An early European explorer travelling through the area reported in 1802 that an estimated 10000 people were gathered there. A productive eel-farming industry existed nearby at Menangle and such a reliable food source must have been needed to sustain so many guests. The eels were smoked in old tree hollows to cook and preserve them. In some nearby sites – former Aboriginal travelling routes – very old medicinal plants and some plants native to other regions of the south-east still record the movement of people to and fro, according to the descendants of the D'harawal.

Today, the Mount Annan area is fast becoming residential. Mount Annan itself is in reality a small hill that sits within Australia's largest garden, the Mount Annan Botanic Garden, devoted to the study and cultivation of native flora. While little evidence remains there of D'harawal society, one colourful story associated with two of its trees was recorded in 2000 by historian Sue Rosen and placed on public record as part of the New South Wales Heritage Office's State Heritage Inventory. Rosen's informants were Frances Bodkin and Gavin Andrews; the Bodkin–Andrews families had inherited the story as members of the D'harawal nation.

The story long predates European settlement, as did one of the trees – the Dooligah Tree – a big kurrajong tree that stood for more than 500 years on the north face of Mount Annan. Beside it grew the Kuritja Tree, a venerable banksia. They are the focus of a legend about hairy men called Watun Goori, an instructive story used to teach children the law and to obey their parents. Here's an abridged version:

> Long ago, the D'harawa'goori were the keepers of the land, the people known today as the D'harawal. They lived here with the Wattun Goori, hairy men who came in two very different kinds: the Dooligah were giants the size of trees and their pint-sized brothers were the Kuritja. They all lived together peacefully for a very long time. On special occasions they would dance together, although the poor little Kuritjas would have to dodge the Dooligahs' big feet.
>
> Then a terrible drought dried up the rivers and waterholes and killed many plants and animals. The D'harawals got by eating plant roots and tubers. Being so small, the Kuritjas survived on flower nectar. But the poor Dooligahs became very, very hungry.

D'harawal culture was rich in tree stories

Trees with spirit

One day, some Dooligahs watched as a mob of D'harawals came by, the grownups chatting away while they searched for juicy roots. Some of the children had disobeyed their parents and lagged behind, making noise and hiding in the bushes. As one Dooligah watched, his stomach rumbled and his mouth watered. Gesturing silence to his companions, he crept up and grabbed three children, burying their faces in his long hair to stifle their screams. Back in his cave he ate the fattest child, keeping the other two for later. His companions then followed and snatched more errant children.

When they noticed some children missing the alarmed D'harawals searched high and low, but found just one clue – a Wattun Goori hair hanging from a branch. When they saw this, the Kuritjas immediately suspected the Dooligahs. Going to their cave, the little men slipped past the sleeping Dooligahs and rescued the captive children.

The overjoyed D'harawals thanked the Kuritjas with gifts of flowers and honey. Soon, though, the children began to forget their lesson and began to stray again. The Dooligahs waited, drooling with anticipation. One day the Kuritjas saw the D'harawal painting their faces and bodies, sharpening their weapons and decorating their shields for battle.

The Kuritjas knew a war would kill many innocent people, so they hatched a peace plan. They told the Dooligahs about the kurrajong tree. In those days all kurrajongs were hollow and even in the worst drought the roots always contained plenty of water and the branches bore many seeds. The little men led their brothers to some kurrajongs, where the Dooligahs drank and ate their fill and fell asleep in the hollow trunks. The Kuritjas then sealed them in, leaving a small crack for fresh air. The Dooligahs were now safe and war had been averted.

But the Kuritjas still feared that a strong wind or lightning, or some fool with an axe, might topple the trees: the Dooligahs would escape and they would be very, very angry. So the little Kuritjas climbed a nearby tree to keep a vigil over the kurrajongs: they're still there today, making sure the Dooligahs don't get out.

But, just in case the Kuritjas fall asleep, or some foolish man comes along and cuts the tree down, it is always a good idea to behave yourself in the bush, and to always do what your parents say. Just in case.

Like many other Aboriginal legends, this charming story works on many levels. The big kurrajong on Mount Annan had a distinct scar on its trunk and the new wood

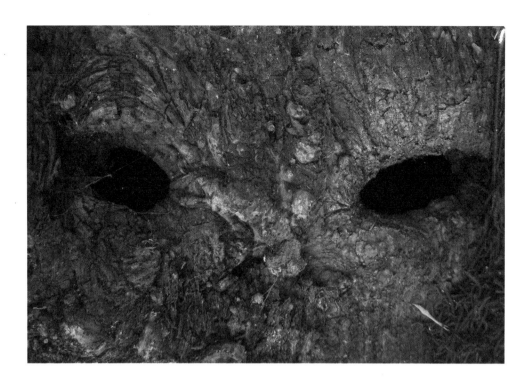

bulging through had dimples and blemishes that, in a child's mind, just might be a horrible Dooligah pressing his face out, waiting to escape. On the nearby banksia tree, the wooden seed cones sitting upright on their branches are the little Kuritja.

No doubt the story has other meanings known only to D'harawal people, but it is a memorable way to teach not only obedience but practical information. Kurrajong roots do indeed yield potable water. Kurrajong seeds can be eaten raw or, when roasted, used to make a coffee-like drink. Its seedling stems can be roasted and eaten as well. Strong 'hairy' fibres stripped from the trunk can be used to make twine and fishing nets. Generations of graziers have also learned to maintain kurrajongs on their land: when pastures are scant during droughts, the leaves of this marvellous tree make palatable and nutritious feed for hungry livestock.

Unfortunately, this tale has an unhappy twist: strong winds swept across Mount Annan in August 2001, and the grand old kurrajong was indeed blown down. Gardens staff told me it had been suffering from the ill-effects of land-clearing around it in earlier times, before the gardens were established in 1988. It had been getting special care and seemed to be responding but the strong winds proved to be too much, too soon. Its great weight ripped its roots from the ground. It was not removed, however: a post-and-rail fence was erected around it and today its slowly disintegrating corpse is used respectfully as an educational display, an example of the process of natural decay. And, yes, the little Kuritja are still there keeping watch. Just in case.

The Prison Tree

DERBY, WESTERN AUSTRALIA

One of the last major frontiers of first contact between traditional Aboriginal Australians and the advancing wave of new settlers was in the continent's north-west in the late 1800s. One stark reminder of how this happened, and how recent it was, stands near the coastal town of Derby. It is a large boab tree, with a typically bulbous shape and the scarecrow limbs that give the species – and its African cousins, the baobabs – its nickname as the upside-down tree.

This one is known as the Prison Tree and serves as a reminder that early meetings of black and white cultures were far from peaceful. Just off the main road into Derby, the tree is a grim but popular stop for tourists, but it is problematical for historians, with claim and counter-claim about the veracity of the reputation attached to it. Both this tree and another less accessible boab – also called the Prison Tree, but formerly known as the Hillgrove Lockup – near Wyndham, 900 kilometres to the north, are reputed to have been used in historic times as overnight cells for Aboriginal prisoners being taken to Derby. There was active and armed resistance to the settlers from many Aborigines and those conflicts and the killing of cattle could bring swift and harsh retribution. Alleged offenders were often marched long distances to nearby towns to face court or jail.

Both the Prison Tree and the Hillgrove Lockup are immense trees with hollow centres and a large opening to the outside in their flanks. The Hillgrove Lockup reportedly could hold ten men. The Prison Tree, with a girth of almost fifteen metres, is said to have been able to accommodate up to twenty men and at one stage was fitted with an iron grate to lock them inside. It is very old, but since these trees lack growth rings no one can say for sure – suggestions that the Prison Tree is 1500 years

Trees with spirit

old seem fanciful, since no boab or baobab is thought to exceed 1000 years in age. One old photograph shown on a noticeboard near the Derby Prison Tree shows a white man on horseback posing in front of a boab. Lined up beside him is a line of mainly young Aboriginal men wearing loincloths – fifteen or so are visible – each fitted with a metal neck-collar that is chained to the man next to him. It is an appalling image – reminiscent of the African slave trade – and there is no denying the brutality of the times and the harsh nature of their restraint. Given that their prisoners were so firmly bound to each other, why would it have been necessary to confine them within the tree, rather than simply attaching the chains to it? Perhaps the tree was used occasionally to confine some prisoners, when police were not the captors. No written historical records are known to verify it. The text accompanying the photograph states:

Derby Prison Tree noticeboard: young Aboriginal men in chains

Before Derby was established in 1883, Aboriginal people were kidnapped from the West Kimberley. The kidnappers, known as blackbirders, were settlers who were connected with the pearling industry. They wanted divers and workers for the pearling boats. They rounded people up, put them in chains and marched them to the coast. Some may have held their captives at the Boab Prison Tree while they waited for a boat. Early pastoralists helped the blackbirders because they thought that removing the young men would guarantee peaceful behaviour from the older ones left behind. The Aboriginal people resisted. A settler named Anthony Cornish was killed in December 1882. Police then came from Roebourne and took more people away. By 1887, the government had built a gaol at Derby (near the present Numbala Nanga site) about five kilometres from the Prison Tree. Over the following decades hundreds of Aboriginal people were held in the original gaol and in one that was built closer to the jetty in 1906. Most of them had been charged with killing and eating livestock.

The prisoners who passed the Prison Tree on their way to Derby came from as far away as Fitzroy Crossing and Christmas Creek. They were forcibly marched between 24 and 48 kilometres a day. One can only wonder at the dismay, dislocation, fear

If Trees Could Speak

Australia's boab trees

Australia's boab trees are closely related to the baobabs of Madagascar and Africa: indeed, they are one of eight species of trees all in the same genus *Adansonia*. They are large bloated trees that revel in hot dry landscapes – thanks to their capacity to store water reserves – and they have soft fibrous wood and large fruits. They are named after the young French naturalist, Michel Adans, who nearly fell out of his canoe when his local guides in Senegal back in 1749 showed him some grand old 'calabash' trees, as he called them.

Six species of baobabs occur in Madagascar, while Africa and Australia have one each (only in Australia are they called boabs). That odd distribution pattern made botanists suspect that they may have originated in the ancient southern supercontinent of Gondwana before it broke up 60 million years ago. But more recent genetic studies suggest that the genus is much younger, first appearing no more than 17 million years ago. Since Madagascar has the most species, it's now thought they evolved there.

It's a short hop from Madagascar to Africa but how did these puffed-up behemoths make it to Australia? The accepted answer today is that they sailed here: their giant seed pods are likely to have been carried east millions of years ago on the ocean currents and trade winds that later brought unwary Dutch explorers crashing into Australia's west coast.

Their distribution within Australia suggests that their first landing point was somewhere in the north-west, from where they have since spread across much of the north, no doubt aided and abetted by animals – and later people – to evolve their own local adaptations. Their capacity to hoard water within their fibrous wood – one huge baobab in South Africa, for example, has an estimated water storage capacity of 113 000 litres – probably was their greatest asset when they got here. Despite their rumpled, warty skin, weird growth habits and obese tendencies, few would argue that these prize graduates from the ugly school of botany are anything but welcome and spectacular additions to the Australian landscape.

Once fitted with an iron grate, the tree could accommodate twenty men

and humiliation they must have felt as they endured these treks and pondered their fate. The Prison Tree is now fenced off from visitors, partly to protect its roots from being compacted and partly to deter the inevitable vandals and thoughtless tourists who delight in carving their names and other messages into the soft wood of these extraordinary trees. The fence is also there because the Prison Tree is officially designated as an Aboriginal Site of Significance. Signage there explains that this is not only for its association with those terrible early times but because of a prior religious significance attached to the tree itself. When explorer Herbert Basedow visited it in 1916 he reported that he saw inside the tree many bleached bones that appeared to be human, including a skull with a bullet hole in it. If this was a mortuary tree, the thought of confining anyone in such a place is abhorrent, but doubly so for people who regarded it as a sacred place for the dead.

Many other boabs across the north-west are a constant source of wonder and often amusement for travellers, due to their elephantine proportions and their often bizarre shapes reminiscent of other things. There are countless teapots along with others suggestive of Darwin stubbies, beer bellies, giant cow pats, mutant hedgehogs, bloated cane toads and even a dead ringer for Fred Flintstone. One on Mount Hart Station in the Kimberley is claimed to be an incredible 27 metres in girth. If so, it beats Australia's so-called 'largest boab tree in captivity' at a caravan park in Wyndham, with a girth of 25 metres. Both of these, however, are mere piglets when measured against the largest baobabs in other lands, a number of which are real porkers exceeding 30 metres in girth.

The Fairies Tree

MELBOURNE, VICTORIA

I have carved in a tree in the Fitzroy Gardens for you, and the fairies, but mostly for the fairies and those who believe in them, for they will understand how necessary it is to have a fairy sanctuary – a place that is sacred and safe as a home should be to all living creatures.

Ola Cohn

Generations of Melbourne children have been taken – or have dragged their parents – to see the Fairies Tree in Fitzroy Gardens. It is just a dead stump but, oh, so much more than just a dead stump. It is a 'gift to the children of Melbourne', beautifully carved and brightly painted with a weird and wonderful assortment of native animals interspersed with quaint fairies, elves and pixies. It was created by Ola Cohn, a noted local sculptor, between 1931 and 1934, Victoria's Centenary Year. It must rate as Australia's most charming public artwork and certainly is one of its best loved. You can see why when you find Cohn's name and those dates carved on one side of the tree: they are just above a wonderful wrinkled fold in the trunk, within which is carved a blond-haired fairy girl holding a swaddled infant on her lap, with three elves huddled around in admiration. It is a twee but delicate homage to a nativity scene.

Indeed, the detail of Cohn's work is a large part of its appeal, no matter how quirky her choice of subject matter. Using the lumps, bumps, creases and grain of the wood, Cohn has created a literally fabulous intermingling of fairytale and fauna. Birds, bats, spiders, lizards, kangaroos and emus entwine with cheeky little fantasy folk with Mr Spock ears and wings growing from their backs. Here a curly-tailed possum hangs beside a quizzical koala, joined on their perches by a group of watching elves wearing

Trees with spirit

green jumpsuits and pointed red caps, plus what appears to be a flying rabbit. There a laughing kookaburra is ringed by fairies, watched from below by a lyrebird. A winged fairy girl stares out stern-faced, one hand aloft to shade her eyes, as if searching for a naughty child. The whole scene is embraced by a large brown eagle with outspread wings. It's a mishmash of cultures, a kind of Peter Pan meets Bib and Bub. But in its own funny sentimental way it works, connecting Europe and Australia, fantasy and reality, past and present, people with nature.

Regardless of its artistic and cultural merits, small kids love it. It's fun. It sparks their imagination. Most of the figures are carved at their eye-level and, best of all, the trunk has a secret hollow where they can leave written wishes for the fairies. Even today, more than 70 years after it was carved, the hollow in the Fairies Tree routinely attracts many gifts of flowers and written notes: some are scrawled spontaneously on scraps of found paper, others are carefully composed and illustrated and brought from home. When I last visited the tree, the note atop the pile was just visible: it featured an excellent drawing of a kangaroo beneath a tree and, in a child's handwriting, one sentence of plain, selfless hope and goodwill:

'A wish for all my family, their health and happiness, Anna'. Melbourne City Council's Lord Mayor, John So, told an ABC radio interviewer in 2005 that council staff 'find it difficult to answer some of the letters. Many of them are quite emotional'.

Ola Cohn's inspiration for the work appears to have the been the Elfin Oak in London's Kensington Gardens. That old stump was likewise sculpted by children's book illustrator Ivor Innes between 1928 and 1930, at a time when Cohn was studying in London at the Royal College of Art. Innes decorated his stump with brightly painted

Trees with spirit

Ola Cohn

Carola Cohn was born in Bendigo on 25 April 1892 and died on 23 December 1964. Known as Ola, she was an influential sculptor and author. She attended art classes at Bendigo School of Mines and later studied at Swinburne Technical College. In 1926 she carved 'Head of a Virgin', which was considered very modern in Australia at the time and is now in the National Gallery of Victoria. In that same year she went to London to attend the Royal College of Art, where her lecturers included the brilliant sculptor Henry Moore. Returning to Melbourne in 1930, she set up a studio at 9 Collins Street and broke new ground for women sculptors by exhibiting her work. She carved the Fairies Tree between 1931 and 1934, and later taught art at Geelong Church of England Grammar School.

In 1937 she moved her studio to a former Cobb and Co. coach house and stables at 41 Gipps Street, East Melbourne, which became a mecca for women sculptors and artists. In 1952, she was awarded the Crouch Prize at Ballarat for her woodcarving 'Abraham'. In 1953, at the age of 61, she married Herbert Green. She was President of the Melbourne Society of Women Painters and Sculptors from 1948 to 1964 and was awarded an OBE for her services to art. Her sculptures in bronze and freestone can be seen in many galleries around Australia. In Adelaide, you can see her wistful limestone statue for the Pioneer Women's Memorial Garden. She bequeathed her studio and a collection of her works to the Council of Education, now the Ola Cohn Memorial Centre. She wrote three books: *The Fairies' Tree*; *More about the Fairies' Tree*; and *Castles in the Air*.

animals, elves and fairies depicting 'the world of the Little People; of Wookey the witch, with her three jars of health, wealth and happiness; of Huckleberry the gnome, carrying a bag of berries up the Gnomes' Stairway to the banquet within Bark Hall; of Grumples and Groodles the Elves being woken up by Brownie, Dinkie, Rumplelocks and Hereandthere stealing eggs from the crows' nest'.

The Elfin Oak has another Australian connection: the late and great comedian Spike Milligan paid for its restoration in the mid-1960s, and came to its rescue again three decades later when he launched a successful campaign for a second restoration. In 1997 it officially became one of England's oddest historic structures when it was formally added to the heritage list of 'buildings of special architectural or historic interest'.

Melbourne's Fairies Tree is likewise listed on the National Trust of Australia (Victoria) Register of Significant Trees, with the following entry:

> As is stated in Ken Scarlett's book *Australian Sculptors*, on page 119, 'It may make a very doubtful claim to being called sculpture, but it can without doubt claim more spectators than any piece of sculpture in Melbourne'. From the early 1930s the work captured the attention of the press and of the general public and very quickly became widely known … It has taken on a sentimental significance which ensures that the work will be preserved as long as possible (making allowance for its vulnerable position, exposed to the elements).

Decay in an artwork like this is inevitable. The trunk came from a large river red gum – probably centuries old and predating European settlement of Australia – that had died of natural causes before it got its makeover. When suggestions were made by Melbourne City Council in 2005 that no more messages should be placed in the hollow, allegedly because they made it more prone to decay, there was public outrage. Its suggested alternative of a wishing well or a post box received a lukewarm reception.

The sawn-off top of the stump is capped to deter rainwater but it stands out in all weathers. Because it has its own fenced enclosure, children have to cross that barrier to leave their notes and flowers in the hollow – when doing so, they can't resist touching the painted figures. Understandably, the tree's exposure has meant that it has required several restorations over the years. It was repaired and repainted in 1998. In 1977 it was extracted from the ground for chemical treatment and the removal of rotted wood, then remounted on a concrete slab. Remarkably, during that process a mummified brushtail possum was found hidden within the trunk: it had been there all that time, perfectly preserved as if by magic.

Trees with spirit

The Faithfull Tree
BENALLA, VICTORIA

In late 1837 a group of eighteen stockmen and convicts led by William Pitt Faithfull set out from the Hunter Valley, in New South Wales to drove a large flock of sheep to newly explored grazing country in Victoria. At one point the party split up and on 11 April 1838, a group led by overseer John Bentley camped by a creek near what is now Benalla. History records that they were set upon in a surprise attack by a large group of Aboriginal men, almost certainly members of the Yorta-Yorta people. Even though the whites were armed with guns, they were outnumbered and overwhelmed by a much larger force of Aborigines, who used their spears and clubs to great and deadly effect. At least eight – some reckon fourteen – of the drovers and one of the Aborigines were killed.

The attack is thought to have been in revenge for an earlier offence against the Yorta-Yorta, but it was not understood by the settlers in that way and harsh reprisals and counter-reprisals followed for some years. The Faithfull Creek massacre made its way into fiction in *The Recollections of Geoffry Hamlyn*, Henry Kingsley's best-selling 1859 novel. On a dark night, a doctor is being led through the bush to tend to someone in a remote place, and asks his guide – Macdonald, a shepherd of Scottish descent – if he knows any ghost stories. The shepherd asks the doctor if he'd ever heard how Faithfull's lot were murdered by the blacks up on the Merrimerangbong.

'This is how it happened: When Faithfull came to take up his country across the mountains yonder, they were a strong party, enough to have been safe in any country, but whether it was food was scarce, or whether it was on account of getting water, I don't know, but they separated, and fifteen of them got into the Yackandandah country before the others.

'Well, you see, they were pretty confident, being still a strong mob, and didn't set any watch or take any care. There was one among them (Cranky Jim they used to call him – he has told me this yarn – he used to be about Reid's mill last year) who always was going on at them to take more care, but they never heeded him at all.

'They found a fine creek, with plenty of feed and water, and camped at it to wait till the others came up. They saw no blacks, nor heard of any, and three days were past, and they began to wonder why the others had not overtaken them.

'The third night they were all sitting round the fire, laughing and smoking, when they heard a loud co'ee on the opposite side of the scrub, and half-a-dozen of them started up, and sang out, "There they are!"

'Well, they all began co'eeing again, and they heard the others in reply, apparently all about in the scrub. So off they starts, one by one, into the scrub, answering and hallooing, for it seemed to them that their mates were scattered about, and didn't know where they were. Well, as I said, fourteen of them started into the scrub, to collect the party and bring them up to the fire; only old Cranky Jim sat still in the camp. He believed, with the others, that it was the rest of their party coming up, but he soon began to wonder how it was that they were so scattered. Then he heard one of them scream, and then it struck him all at once that this was a dodge of the blacks to draw the men from the camp, and, when they were abroad, cut them off one by one, plunder the drays, and drive off the sheep.

'So he dropped, and crawled away in the dark. He heard the co'ees grow fewer and fewer as the men were speared one by one, and at last everything was quiet, and then he knew he was right, and he rose up and fled away.

'In two days he found the other party, and told them what had happened. They came up, and there was some sharp fighting, but they got a good many of their sheep back.

'They found the men lying about singly in the scrub, all speared. They buried them just where they found each one, for it was hot weather. They buried them four-foot deep, but they wouldn't lie still.

'Every night, about nine o'clock, they get up again, and begin co'eeing for an hour or more. At first there's a regular coronach of them, then by degrees the shouts get fewer and fewer, and, just when you think it's all over, one will break out loud and clear close to you, and after that all's still again.

Trees with spirit

'You don't believe that story, I suppose?'

'If you press me very hard,' said the doctor, 'I must confess, with all humility, that I don't!'

'No more did I,' said Macdonald, 'till I heard 'em!'

'Heard them!' said the doctor.

'Ay, *and seen them*!' said the man, stopping and turning round.

'You most agreeable of men! Pray, tell me how.'

'Why, you see, last year I was coming down with some wool-drays from Parson Dorken's, and this Cranky Jim was with us, and told us the same yarn, and when he had finished, he said, "You'll know whether I speak truth or not to-night, *for we're going to camp at the place where it happened.*"

'Well, and so we did, and, as well as we could reckon, it was a little past nine when a curlew got up and began crying. That was the signal for the ghosts, and in a minute they were co'eeing like mad all round. As Jim had told us, one by one ceased until all was quiet, and I thought it was over, when I looked, and saw, about a hundred yards off, a tall man in grey crossing a belt of open ground. He put his hand to his mouth, gave a wild shout, and disappeared!'

'Thank you,' said the doctor.

A large river red gum once marked the massacre site. It was photographed in 1907, when it was apparently already dead, with the words 'Faithfull Tree' painted on its trunk. The photographs were said to show a policeman displaying the fractured skull of one of the dead from a grave beside the tree, where several victims had been buried. The Faithfull Tree is no more, but a granite boulder and memorial plaque mark the site.

The explorers' trees

The Carstensz Tree

CAPE YORK, QUEENSLAND

In early 1623, officials of the Dutch East India Company in Java dispatched two yachts – *Pera* and *Arnhem* – to investigate a possible shipping route between New Guinea and Australia, now known as Torres Strait. They knew that Torres, a Spaniard, had mapped much of the southern New Guinea coast in 1606. That was the same year that Willem Jansz in the *Duyfken* had made the first documented European discovery of the Australian mainland; that was also the first definite contact between Aborigines and white people, on Cape York Peninsula, which ended in a bloody clash in which a Dutch seaman died on the banks of the Wenlock River.

The skipper of the *Pera* was Jan Carstensz and his task was to learn if Torres and Jansz really had discovered separate lands, with open water between them. Carstensz's journal records that the voyagers sighted Cape York Peninsula on 12 April 1623, and over the next fortnight mapped its west coast. Several landing parties were involved in skirmishes with Aborigines, one of whom was captured and later taken back to Batavia. Carstensz wrote that he saw not even one 'fruit-bearing tree, nor anything that man could make use of . . . this is the most arid and barren region that could be found anywhere on the earth; the inhabitants, too, are the most wretched and poorest creatures that I have seen'. For a man in search of gold, silver and spices, it was clearly a bitter disappointment. He did see fit, however, to commemorate their visit at a site near the base of the Gulf of Carpentaria, by the mouth of the Staaten River. There he fixed a tablet to a tree, inscribed with the date – 24 April 1623 – and a declaration that the two ships had come on behalf of the 'High and Mighty Lords States General' of Batavia. The tablet has vanished. Nothing is known of the identity of the tree selected

by Carstensz for his historic act, but we can say that it was probably the first Australian tree ever to be used by white men as a memorial.

Since then, trees by the thousand have served to mark important Australian places, events and people, the travels of explorers, and births, deaths and marriages. That was true from the very first days of British contact with the continent. An inscription was made on a tree at Botany Bay in 1770, for example, recording the ship's name and date of the visit there by James Cook in the *Endeavour*. It had apparently disappeared before the arrival of the First Fleet eighteen years later. Only a few weeks afterwards, on 17 February 1788, Father Receveur – the Franciscan friar who served as naturalist and astronomer with the French explorer La Perouse on the *Astrolabe* – died and was buried at Botany Bay, his gravesite marked by an inscribed board nailed to a tree. As a mark of respect, Governor Phillip had the board replaced by an inscribed copper plate, but that has been lost to history. Receveur's grave is marked now by a suitable memorial and is still visited by French sailors wishing to pay their respects.

The explorers' trees

The Investigator Tree

SWEERS ISLAND, QUEENSLAND

One remarkable historic tree with important commemorative inscriptions stood for many years on Sweers Island in the Gulf of Carpentaria. It became known as the Investigator Tree because that word had been carved into it in large letters by Matthew Flinders in 1802, during his outstanding circumnavigation of Australia in the dodgy old sloop *Investigator*. In 1841, Lieutenant John Lort Stokes, commander of the even more famous British ship HMS *Beagle*, visited the island and found 'the name of Flinders' ship cut on a tree . . . and still perfectly legible although nearly forty years old'. Excited, he wrote: 'It was . . . our good fortune to find at last some traces of the *Investigator*'s voyage, which at once invested the place with all the charms of association, and gave it an interest in our eyes that words can ill express. All the adventures and sufferings of the intrepid Flinders vividly recurred to our memory.' Stokes carved the *Beagle*'s name there as well. Subsequent explorers added more names, including vessels and people associated with Augustus Gregory's 1856 North Australian Expedition and William Landsborough's 1861 expedition in search of Burke and Wills.

After a severe cyclone was judged to have mortally wounded the tree in 1887, part of its trunk was removed and taken in 1889 to the Queensland Museum. By that time it carried many names, mostly illegible, and there was even much speculation – and that appears to have been all it was – that it also carried Dutch and Chinese inscriptions older than the Flinders one. In 1901, the Northern Protector of Aborigines, Dr Walter Roth, visited Sweers Island and reported that this 'very interesting historical landmark' had been vandalised and all that remained was one post of a fence that formerly protected it.

The remains of the Investigator Tree are now held at the Museum of Lands

Surveying and Mapping, in Brisbane, a branch of Queensland Museum. A wooden plug taken from it identified it as the handsome but little-known native hackberry tree, *Celtis paniculata*. In 1988, as part of a Bicentennial project, museum staff obtained a seedling of that species grown by native plant enthusiasts from seed collected in the Ipswich region. The seedling was taken to Sweers Island and, with the help of surveyors, it was planted in the place of the original. A plaque marks the site.

The Investigator Tree was famous for recording many explorers' visits dating back to 1802

The explorers' trees

The Dig Tree

COOPER CREEK, QUEENSLAND

> I have only one ambition, which is to do some deed before I die, that shall entitle me to have my name honourably inscribed on the page of history. If I succeed in that I care not what death, or when I die.
>
> Robert O'Hara Burke

His aim was to become famous, even if it killed him, and he succeeded. Even though few Australians now regard him as a hero, history has still been much too kind to Robert O'Hara Burke. He certainly got his name written on history's page, forever linked to that of the surveyor William John Wills, his far more competent partner in exploration. The one word that summons up their ghosts is carved in capital letters – DIG – inscribed on a living tree.

Thanks to its intimate association with the 1860 Burke and Wills expedition, the Dig Tree is arguably Australia's most famous individual tree. It is a graceful coolibah that grows in an arid, ancient landscape in south-west Queensland, near the South Australian border. It has its own special reserve within the boundaries of Nappa Merrie cattle station, 1200 kilometres west of Brisbane, and its ownership is officially vested in the Royal Queensland Historical Society. Despite its remote location, tens of thousands of people make the pilgrimage along the famous Birdsville and Strzelecki tracks every year to visit this tree, a shrine to one of the most memorable and sorry events in the history of exploration.

Happily, the Dig Tree is alive and well and, despite being an estimated 350 years old, looks to have many decades of life left in it yet. It stands on the banks of Cooper Creek, a beautiful watery oasis that brims with life. The creek forms part of the

sprawling drainage basin that occasionally takes monsoonal floods down through the Channel Country into the Lake Eyre Basin. Queenslanders have a joke that it takes two rivers to make a creek: in this case, the Thomson and Barcoo rivers join to form Cooper Creek. The tree is well placed for survival: even in dry times this 60-kilometre section of the Cooper – from Nappa Merrie to Innamincka – carries water in a single deep channel that flows between rocky hills. It is more like a giant permanent billabong than a conventional river.

Australia's most famous individual tree: the Dig Tree at Cooper Creek

How Burke and Wills contrived to die here – surrounded by natural riches and food and water aplenty – is an incredible tale. It is so well told by Sarah Murgatroyd in her brilliant book, *The Dig Tree*, that I can do no better than direct you to that if you

The explorers' trees

want a comprehensive account of their expedition. Murgatroyd's own sad fate – she died of cancer at the age of 35, just a few weeks after the book was published – has added yet another layer of sadness to the tale. To understand the pivotal role the Dig Tree plays in the story, however, we must revisit the events that led Burke and Wills to it.

The tragedy really began in 1860, when the learned gentlemen of the Exploration Committee of Victoria's Royal Society decided to appoint Burke to lead an expedition with the aim of crossing Australia from south to north. It was to be the most extravagantly equipped and heavily financed journey of exploration in colonial Australia. It was to go where no maps existed and it was to have a serious crack at one of the most ambitious journeys of its kind ever attempted.

With all this at stake, 'the idea of Burke leading any expedition anywhere was ludicrous', says Murgatroyd. He could hardly read a compass, he had no natural bush sense and was infamous for his uncanny ability to get lost even on his way home. More to the point, he had no exploring experience nor had he ever travelled beyond the colony's settled districts. His temperament for leadership was seriously deficient, he was disorganised, impetuous and lacked composure under duress. He had intelligence, great passion and energy, to be sure, but he was at heart a gambler with a long track record of losing bets.

But Burke was a charmer. A bushy-bearded, blue-eyed Irishman, he radiated a masculinity that women found alluring and men found beguiling. His family background in the Irish gentry bestowed no wealth on him but he was well educated in literature, languages and music. As a young man his family connections scored him a place in the Austrian Army, where he quickly established a pattern of gambling, drinking and womanising. An honour duel fought over a woman left him with a large scar on his cheek. He went absent without leave at one point to avoid heavy gambling debts, only escaping a court martial in 1848 when an inquiry found that his debts were the result of 'carelessness', not deceit, and allowed him to resign in dishonour. He returned home and joined the Irish Constabulary, where his strength and athleticism were much admired. But boredom set in and tales of gold and opportunity brought him to Melbourne in 1853. His timing was bad. The best of the gold rush was over and, with nuggets as scarce as experienced police, Burke soon had to return to uniform as an acting inspector at Beechworth.

His career there was far from exemplary: he was bored, his appearance was almost always unkempt, he was chided by magistrates for his lax paperwork and he gained a reputation as an eccentric for his habit of spending hours soaking in a bathtub of water in his garden, cursing the summer heat and the mosquitoes. Between bouts of

indolence came bursts of frenzied activity that saw Burke chop down trees and take long walks: he confided to a colleague that he desperately wanted to do 'something to take the sting out of him'. The death of his brother James in 1854 – the first British officer killed in the Crimean War – deeply affected him. He later sailed to England to join the army, but once again his timing was bad: the war had finished and a peace treaty had been signed. He returned to Australia and resumed his former life, the sting still inside him.

No matter how much he wanted the job, why was someone so spectacularly incompetent and unqualified chosen to lead the expedition? When he moved to Castlemaine in 1858, Burke met and helped a prominent but dubious railway tycoon, John Bruce, who in turn introduced him to Melbourne society. Burke's family and military background, his personal charm and the nature of his brother's gallant death in the Crimean War gave him a cachet that resonated well with the class-conscious members of the Melbourne Club. They

The idea of Burke leading any exploration anywhere was ludicrous

admitted him as a member and somehow overlooked the warning signs as he once again ran up large gambling debts. With such influential backers, Burke was happy to put his name forward when contenders to lead the expedition were sought. To cut a long story short, snobbery, scheming, bickering, factionalism and incompetence on the part of the Exploration Committee ensured that the best candidates were excluded. In the end, Burke was the last man left standing.

The idea for the expedition had been around for several years, originally with a more scientific purpose and to search for the missing Leichhardt expedition. The discovery of gold in the 1850s had given the young nation a heady dose of growth fever. With this new-found material wealth, the colonists set out to realise what until then had only been dreams. One dream was to 'open up the interior' of the continent, two-thirds of which remained unexplored by the settlers at the time. There lay the potential, they fondly hoped, for important discoveries and perhaps even greater riches – an inland sea, vast new grazing lands or even another booty of gold. As the decade wore on, a sense of competitive urgency grew between Victorians and South Australians, in particular, to reach out and claim the continent's north.

A series of expeditions had already been sent into the interior. Edward Eyre had found a chain of salt lakes and a 'dreary waste' beyond the Flinders Ranges. Charles Sturt had tried to reach the centre by travelling up the Murray and Darling rivers and cutting north across the desert, but he was trapped by drought. Later, in 1845, Sturt found the main watercourses leading into Lake Eyre: Cooper Creek, Eyre Creek and the Georgina River. Yet the disappearance of Ludwig Leichhardt's 1848 expeditionary team – while attempting to cross the continent from east to west – was an ominous sign. That party consisted of 7 men, 50 cattle, 270 goats, 7 horses and tons of supplies, yet it vanished without trace.

But in 1856, surveyor Augustus Gregory – arguably Australia's most successful explorer – travelled without mishap from north-western Australia to Brisbane. In 1858, after being sent to search for Leichhardt, Gregory crossed from the Darling Downs in Queensland to South Australia by following the Cooper and Strzelecki creeks. Good sense and good luck had been on his side. Country that was parched and barren in one season could be a sea of green in the next. Where one explorer found an 'earthly hell', another found a 'paradise on earth'.

In 1859 the redoubtable John McDouall Stuart found a series of springs and waterholes that sparked a rush of new pastoral runs across the south of Lake Eyre. Stuart was a fine explorer, whose journeys in time paved the way for the building of the overland telegraph to Darwin and a major railway line. For now, however, the country further north remained a blank. But graziers were enticed by an 1841 report from the Beagle's voyage of well-grassed land between two rivers on the coast of the Gulf of Carpentaria, marked intriguingly on maps of the day as The Plains of Promise.

The Royal Society's expedition plan suddenly took on a greater urgency in August 1859, when South Australia offered a prize of 2000 pounds for the 'first person who shall succeed in crossing the country lately discovered by Mr Stuart, to either the north or north-western shore of the Australian continent, west of the 143rd degree of longitude'. Victorians made rich by gold were restless to make their mark on the nation and this was another prize worth seeking. Not to be outdone, Victoria's chief secretary, William Nicholson, announced in January 1860 that parliament would fund an expedition to the tune of 6000 pounds. In March 1860 Stuart set out on his first attempt to make the south-north crossing of the continent. He made it two-thirds of

The explorers' trees

the way, to Tennant Creek, before being forced to turn back.

So it was that on 20 August 1860, some 15 000 Melburnians – one-eighth of the city's population – turned out to cheer on the extraordinary departure of the Victorian exploring party. Burke's orders made it clear that this was to be a straight-out race against South Australia to stake out land claims in the north. A circus atmosphere prevailed at the biggest, most chaotic farewell bash of its kind the nation had yet seen. Tents, horses, American-style wagons and box after box of equipment were scattered around Melbourne's Royal Park, with a steadily growing crowd milling about amid the expeditionary team's efforts to pack. The 27 camels – a special innovation at the time – were star attractions, attended by exotically dressed 'sepoys' under the command of the equally orientally attired George Landells, Burke's second-in-command. The camels had their own specially made blankets and shoes, and even special airbags to keep their heads above water on river crossings. The scent of these ships of the desert made a horse bolt and throw its rider. A camel in turn broke free and scattered a laughing crowd as a portly policeman nimbly fled its path. An impromptu band played and a sly-grog shop operated in some bushes.

'In the centre of the turmoil, standing on top of a wagon, was a tall, flamboyant Irishman, with flashing blue eyes and a magnificent black beard,' says Murgatroyd. 'Shouting orders in a strong Galway accent, he was trying (and failing) to impose order on the mayhem below. Expedition leader Robert O'Hara Burke grew ever more impatient as he tried to squeeze too much equipment onto too few camels, horses and wagons.' Even before they had marched a step, Burke had sacked two men for disobedience and one for drunkenness.

Efforts to cater for all eventualities had lumbered the team with a ridiculous quantity of gear, more than twenty tons of it. One beast was a designated 'hospital camel' with its own enclosed stretcher. Each of the eighteen men wore a scarlet jumper, flannel trousers, a colonial cabbage-tree hat and carried a charcoal filter in his pocket for cleansing drinking water. They carried rockets, coloured lights and a Chinese gong in case anyone got lost. They even had cedar-topped dinner tables and chairs. One of the wagons was designed to be converted into a river punt.

At 4 pm, after a brief awkward speech from Burke, the expedition set off, led by Landells on a huge bull camel and Burke on his favourite horse, a grey named Billy. The portents were not good: several of the wagons became bogged at the edge of the park and another broke down. Once under way, the procession was half a kilometre long.

It must be said that the expedition did eventually reach the north coast, more by good fortune than good management. But that was its only success. Everything else about it was a disastrous failure and for that Burke has the lion's share of responsibility. As one account puts it: 'He was a product of that heroic age of empire which believed that a gentleman of good breeding with a confident military manner and an impressive beard must make an effective leader.' Burdened by a self-defeating strategy – to travel fast while loaded down with copious equipment – Burke compounded his woes by pigheadedness, poor judgment and impatience. He could have reached his first staging point, for example, far quicker and easier by boat along the Darling River. He even had an offer of a free ride on a steam boat, but turned it down for petty political reasons. He chose to slog men and beasts the 750 kilometres overland instead, leaving a trail of bad cheques, ill feeling and much of his equipment along the way. He did not reach the most outlying town, Menindee, until the heat of summer was beginning to make itself felt. He quarrelled with all and sundry, sacked Landells, his deputy, then challenged him to a duel.

Tired of slow progress and fearful that Stuart might steal his thunder, Burke ignored local advice to wait out the summer and instead opted for a radical change of plan. He split his party and took a small group north to Cooper Creek, country already explored by Sturt and Gregory, and established a depot – Camp 65 – by a coolibah tree at the Bulloo Bulloo waterhole. The rest of the team were to follow with the supplies over ensuing weeks, but instead of waiting for the supplies to arrive, Burke again split the team. He left behind three men and supplies in the charge of William Brahe. On 16 December Burke took his horse, six camels, three men and survival rations and plunged headlong into the unknown. It was his biggest gamble yet. It was the height of summer and they were going beyond the furthest known point on the white man's map. Of the three men with him – Wills, the quiet methodical surveyor and replacement deputy; John King, the camel handler; and Charley Gray, a solidly built sailor – only King had experience of the outback. So determined was Burke to travel light that he would not even pack a tent. Their destination was 1500 kilometres away, and then they would have to make the return journey. It was beyond imprudent – it was reckless.

Brahe was told to wait, and if Burke's group had not returned within three months, to assume that they had either perished or diverted to Queensland. Brahe was then to head back to Menindee. Brahe and his men spent the summer by the waterhole, shaded by the coolibah tree. The rear group of the party failed to arrive because Burke had appointed a local man, William Wright, to take charge of it. Wright was left waiting for three months before the incompetent Exploration Committee approved his appointment and made funds available to him. Brahe and the others eked out their supplies, which they protected from over-friendly Aborigines by building a six-metre-

The explorers' trees

square stockade made of saplings: they called it Fort Wills.

Not until he was sure that Burke's team must have run out of food and headed into Queensland did Brahe decide to leave Camp 65. His own men were weak and ill with scurvy and he had overstayed Burke's orders by one month and one week.

On 18 April 1861, he wrote in his journal, 'there is no probability of Mr Burke returning this way', and with his own food running low, he made the decision to leave for Menindee three days later. Just in case Burke should return, Brahe buried an emergency cache of food and supplies in an old camel trunk beneath the tree. He took a knife and cut away a roughly circular portion of the fissured bark on the trunk to reach the heartwood beneath. On it, he deeply notched the word DIG. There is argument – which I won't enter – about other carvings and their meanings. On a nearby branch he cut two dates – those of his arrival and departure.

Meanwhile, Burke's party had been lucky: it was a relatively wet season and they were able to move from waterhole to waterhole through the Channel Country, cross the craggy Selwyn Range and find the Flinders River to take them north. It took eight weeks of hard toil, but on 10 February 1861 they reached tidal salt water in the midst of an impenetrable tangle of mangroves and sticky mud. They came to a halt twenty kilometres short of the Gulf of Carpentaria; they never saw the open sea but were satisfied that they had come close enough to claim success. Yet the cost had been too great: the outward leg had taken two-thirds of the time allotted for the journey there and back, they had consumed three-quarters of their food and they were weak, sick and exhausted. The return trip was a nightmare struggle. They ate Burke's horse and one of the camels but were too frail to hunt the abundant game around them. At one point Gray was caught stealing flour and complained of illness; Burke beat him about the head and accused him of feigning his condition. Gray soon proved him wrong and died on 17 April. The three survivors spent an entire day scraping out a grave for Gray and burying him. Four days later, in a desperate last raw surge of energy and hope, Burke, Wills and King staggered into the empty Camp 65. When they saw the command carved into the coolibah, they dug up the trunk and were aghast to learn from a note inside that Brahe's group had left that very morning. The coals of their fire were still warm. It was appalling bad luck, the cruellest twist of fate.

After feasting on porridge and tea with sugar, Burke made yet another bad call. The very next day they would strike out for Blanchewater station in South Australia, following Gregory's route down the Strzelecki channel. But they could not find the way and were forced to return to Cooper Creek. In yet another cruel twist, on their return journey Brahe's exhausted party had encountered William Wright, at long last bringing up the rear, a fortnight after Brahe had turned for home. Wright and another man immediately rode to Camp 65 to make one last check for signs of life, but Burke's group meanwhile had come and gone. Because they had covered their tracks and any signs of digging – to deter Aborigines – there was no clue that they had been there. Wright scouted around for fifteen minutes and left, unaware that Burke, Wills and King were now only a few kilometres further along the creek.

Friendly Aborigines did their best to help the three men as their strength slowly faded. Too weak to hunt or fish, they gathered and ate plenty of nardoo – a starchy staple food of the Aborigines – but did not know that it needed to be washed and cooked first to remove an enzyme that acts as a vitamin-B blocker. Despite eating several pounds of nardoo a day – which should have kept them alive – the explorers grew weaker and weaker, almost certainly suffering from severe beri-beri, a deficiency of Vitamin B. Already severely malnourished, they were now slowly poisoning themselves. Wills was the first to die, in late June, alone on the banks of the Tilka waterhole, about fifteen kilometres west of where Innamincka now stands. Burke and King tried to follow the creek and seek help from a group of Aborigines. Burke expired a couple of days later, by the Yidniminckanie waterhole. As one writer put it, he died of malnutrition with his revolver in his hand beside a waterhole teeming with birdlife. John King managed to find the Aborigines and survived with them for three more months, when he was found – emaciated, dirty and irretrievably traumatised – by a relief party led by Alfred Howitt.

The expedition had been a disaster from start to finish. Seven men had died. Both Gregory and Leichhardt found safer, more reliable routes into the country that killed Burke: no one followed his route. The best that could be said of the expedition was that it sparked a rush of others, sent out (ostensibly at least) to search for the missing men. Vast new areas of Queensland were explored, the Diamantina River was found and the Gulf was reached several times over, without a man being lost.

Victorians had no profit from Burke's epic journey. In 1862 the Queensland border was shifted west from 141° to 138° longitude, taking in the new-found grazing country. In 1863, South Australia was granted the Northern Territory, taking in all the country to the west of that line, and later it got the Overland Telegraph as well. And yet Melbourne sang Burke's praises in death as if he were a hero, not a dangerous fool. When his and Wills's remains were recovered from the desert, the town threw a funeral even more expansive than their first farewell. Shops and offices were shut and three-quarters of the population turned out for the event, with a cavalcade of funeral carriages and mourners that stretched for several streets and took two and a half hours to reach Melbourne Cemetery. The funeral car itself was a giant carriage five metres long, seven metres high and pulled by a team of six elaborately decorated horses.

The explorers' trees

Their graves were later marked with a 34-ton monolith.

When the Exploration Committee tallied the last of all the bills years later, the expedition's final cost was 57 840 pounds – the equivalent of several millions of dollars in today's money, and five times the original budget. By way of comparison, the British expedition almost a century later that led to the first ascent of Mount Everest, by Edmund Hillary and Tenzing Norgay, cost 20 000 pounds.

On Swanston Street in Melbourne's city centre there is a grand monument to the expedition. Bronze panels attached to a stone plinth tell the story in pictures, complete with the Dig Tree. Atop the plinth sits Wills, writing in a notebook. Towering above all stands the bearded Burke, gazing into the distance.

If he's looking for the Dig Tree, it's still going strong, as is the ranger who cares for it, Alf 'Bomber' Johnston. At 72, Bomber is still a licensed pilot; apart from his ranger duties he is a dab hand at bush mechanics, mending bores and doing general repairs. He's spent 57 years of his life here and knows the tree as well as anyone. When it flowers in early summer, for example, the little buds look 'like boiled eggs sitting in their egg cups', he told me. The boardwalk around the tree was designed to be removed quickly with a forklift when floods are imminent, to avoid damage to the tree. And the Dig Tree has holes drilled in its trunk, into which a systemic insect poison is injected every few years to protect it from termites and leaf-chewing bugs.

Bomber is a fount of stories about life in and around Nappa Merrie, as any tourist who camps there soon discovers. Many are disappointed, he says, that the word DIG can no longer be seen on the tree, only the expeditionary blaze of the letter B – for Burke – and beneath it LXV, for Camp 65. Much admired nearby, though, is another historic tree – the Face Tree – with a carving of Burke on it, a later memorial dating from 1898.

Bomber asks visitors to reflect on the boredom and loneliness endured by Brahe's party as they waited vainly beneath the tree. 'Today, they've got their portable CD players and satellite phones, but those men had nothing like that and they sat it out for four months and one day,' he says. 'If I'm out with a few fellows we're sick of each others' stories within two days. Think what it must have been like for them.'

Most visitors, he says, are very respectful towards the tree and keen to know its history and see it in context with the place. Visitor numbers fluctuate according to the swings of the climate and the economy from year to year. In 2004, about 9500 people came to see the Dig Tree but in 2005 the total was only 6800. Bomber expects the tally to grow as road improvements bring it within easier reach. He first reached the property on horseback but these days you can drive a car on bitumen road all the way from the east coast to within 100 kilometres of the Cooper. As a result, some guests now expect more home comforts and sophisticated services. Bomber says: 'We had this one woman, a big lady, who complained a lot and said she'd been dragged here against her will. She went crook at me and told me I wasn't doing a very good job. When I asked why, she said her mobile phone reception was poor. I told her, "Lady, if I controlled Telstra I can tell you I wouldn't be out here looking after a coolibah tree".'

Somehow, though, I got the feeling that you'd have to prise Bomber away from his Dig Tree and this evocative place.

The explorers' trees

In living
memory

The Tree of Knowledge

BARCALDINE, QUEENSLAND

Famous as the birthplace of the Australian Labor Party, the Tree of Knowledge in the central Queensland town of Barcaldine is a ghost gum with rich historic links. The early 1890s were tense and at times chaotic in Australia. Politics and the economy were at the heart of it. Just as the Federation movement was gathering momentum, a financial crash in Argentina sparked an international economic crisis prompting foreign powers to withdraw their deposits from Australian banks. Depression followed: banks and businesses folded, agricultural produce prices plunged, most public works projects were halted and jobs dried up. Against this backdrop, labour and capital were clashing, especially in the wool industry and on the waterfront. At issue was the right of workers to unionise and the right of employers to choose whether they employed union or non-union labour. Armed troops fired on a mob in Melbourne and a near-riot occurred in Sydney in 1890 when non-unionists transported wool bales under armed escort.

Trouble flared in the bush as well, where shearers worked under terrible conditions, often with inadequate pay. At its 1890 annual conference in Bourke, the Australian Shearers Union voted to ban its members from working with non-unionists and the issue soon sparked strikes in Queensland. Squatters responded by forming their own organisation, the Pastoralists Federal Council. On 5 January 1891, the manager of Logan Downs Station, Charles Fairbain, tried to get his shearers to sign a pastoralists' contract that the shearers would not accept. In a reaction that would shape labour laws and industrial relations for many decades afterwards, the union called a strike. Shearers from many other properties were called off the job and joined the industrial action. Months of high tension and conflict followed. Crops were torched, woolsheds

On the sign:
IT WAS UNDER THE "TREE OF KNOWLEDGE" NEXT TO THE RAILWAY STATION THAT AN ORGANISATION WAS FORMED IN 1891 THAT LATER BECAME THE AUSTRALIAN LABOUR PARTY.

The birthplace in 1891 of the Labor Party: poisoned and killed in 2006

burnt down, armed skirmishes took place and shearers' camps sprang up outside many towns. Armed troops were brought in to protect non-union 'scab' labourers and prominent strikers were arrested. Feelings ran so high that at times it looked as though central Queensland might descend into civil war.

Barcaldine (Barcy for short) was at the centre of the action. On 1 May 1890, one of the world's first May Day marches was held there, with more than 1300 men – half of them mounted on horseback – marching with union banners behind leaders wearing blue sashes and carrying the Eureka Flag. But within weeks, hunger and wet weather had weakened the strikers' resolve and numbers in the camps grew thinner. At Barcaldine, some 120 mounted infantrymen with bayonets drawn were sent in to break the strike. They surrounded the union office and arrested the strike leaders, who were later charged with conspiracy and sedition, and given hefty fines and three-year jail terms. Henry Lawson penned his poem 'Freedom on the Wallaby' in response to these events, with its famous last line about blood staining the wattle.

Workers across Australia soon channelled the foment of the times into electoral success. In 1891, 1892 and 1893 respectively, Labour League and other labour candidates from various parties scored 35 seats in the New South Wales legislative assembly elections, ten seats in Victoria and then fifteen in Queensland. Others won seats in 1893 in South Australia and Tasmania. Out of this movement came the Australian Labor Party (ALP), and the shearers' strike and Barcaldine are credited with inspiring its birth.

Today in Barcaldine you'll find a two-hectare memorial to those events in the form of the Australian Workers' Heritage Centre. There was also the Tree of Knowledge, until recently, growing on the main street where the striking shearers are said to have met to air their feelings and plot their tactics. The tree – a ghost gum thought to be about 150 years old – was thriving after tree surgery and arboristic therapy in 1990. It was the centre of attention for the ALP centenary celebrations in 1991, when Labor Prime Minister Bob Hawke and Queensland Labor Premier Wayne Goss planted saplings grown from cuttings taken from it. Over the years it had termites, gall wasps and dieback, it had been ringbarked by galahs and suffered from compacted soil and even bitumen placed around its base. With ongoing care and attention it might have had another 50 years or so of life left in it.

Unfortunately, while writing this book, news came through that the Tree of Knowledge was ailing. A few weeks before the 2006 May Day march in Barcaldine, locals noticed that the town's best-known resident was unexpectedly dropping some of its leaves. Pat Ogden, the local Labor Party official who had taken a keen interest in the tree over the years, thought the leaf-drop was simply an unusual, but entirely natural, event. By May Day, however, it was clear from the sickly yellow shrubbery surrounding it, that the tree's root zone had been doused with herbicide (probably the common weed killer glyphosate) in a dose large enough to affect even this substantial and well-established gum. Tragically, emergency measures came too late. The tree was bare of leaves and its bark had dehydrated and crazed before flaking off.

'Sadly, it's living up to its name – it's a ghost gum,' Ogden said in one of many media interviews. The famous tree's passing made national news and prompted much comment, debate and reflection. The story came as part of a run of sad events in popular culture – the deaths of iconic Australians Steve Irwin 'the Crocodile Hunter', racing driver Peter Brock and *Storm Boy* author, Colin Thiele.

The Tree of Knowledge certainly did not die by accident or of natural causes, but by a malicious and senseless act of vandalism that is difficult to comprehend. This tree was not only part of Labor's history, but of the cultural heritage of all Australians.

Barcaldine gained many benefits from it, including publicity that resulted in sustained tourist income. Museums and historical displays are one thing, but it is quite another to stand in the shade of the self-same tree that marks the scene of a historic event – in this case as the rallying point for a whole social, industrial and political movement. When those events occurred so long ago, it's also a reminder of the great longevity of trees. We can be thankful that the people of Barcaldine were farsighted enough to take and grow cuttings of the tree while it was still alive – a sensible insurance policy against calamity, natural or otherwise, for any rare and important plant.

I'm puzzled as to why our public agencies – or even our philanthropists – have not done likewise for many of the significant trees detailed in this book. At the time of writing, there is much public debate about the perceived failures in the way history is taught in Australia. Natural history doesn't fare much better. Perhaps the Federal Government could support such a project with public funds, with the offspring of our greatest trees planted as 'living history forests'? It wouldn't cost much and the vivid memory of a visit to one – to be able to see, feel, smell and even hear such trees – would surely stay with a young mind for many years. Can you or your child recognise a coolibah?

I suggested earlier that heritage tree trails could easily be developed around the nation. What better than to have those trails lead to a whole forest of wonderful Australian trees? I hope as well that some enterprising commercial grower reading this might be spurred to develop an Australian Heritage Trees collection. What a marvellous gift such a tree would make, and how satisfying it would be to watch one of our national treasures growing on your own land and know that you were helping to conserve it. As you'll read later, a precious few trees – such as the Wollemi pine – have had this special treatment with good commercial results. Others have been propagated widely not for profit but for valid emotional reasons.

The Lone Pine

MANY LOCATIONS

Lone Pine cemetery, Gallipoli: on the quiet orderly rows of headstones are inscribed the many names of young Australian men who fought and died in one of the bloodiest, hardest and most awful battles in a bloody awful campaign. Burials were brought in from scattered graves and from Brown's Dip North and South Cemeteries, which were behind the Australian trenches of April–August 1915. Buried or commemorated in the lawn cemetery today are 1167 World War I servicemen, almost half of them unidentified. Within the cemetery stands the Lone Pine memorial to more than 4900 Australian and New Zealand servicemen who died in the Anzac area and whose gravesites are unknown.

The single pine tree that graces the site today is not the source of its famous name. That credit goes to a solitary Aleppo pine that stood on that hilly landscape in early 1915, high above Anzac Cove. The area had been clothed with pines, but Turkish forces had cut them down and used the logs to cover their trenches. For reasons unknown, they had left just one pine standing. After the Anzac landings on 25 April, the ridge fell briefly into the hands of Australian forces who called it Lone Pine or Lonesome Pine. War historian Charles Bean saw what he called a 'single dwarf pine tree', but the tree was blasted to pieces by artillery shells within the first few days of fighting. The Turks then retook the ridge and made it a stronghold from May to July; the heavy loss of life there prompted them to name it Kanli Sirt, or Bloody Ridge. But much worse was to come.

At 4.30 pm on 6 August 1915, the 1st Australian Infantry Division launched a major offensive on the ridge. The heaviest of the fighting lasted a mere three days. The ridge was recaptured under extraordinary duress but the victory came at horrendous

cost to both sides. In that short time more than 2000 young Australian men died and the Turks lost a staggering 7000 men. Extraordinary bravery was in equal measure with the bloodshed: Australian soldiers won seven Victoria Crosses in that one battle.

For the first hour, Allied artillery unleashed a bombardment that sent a hail of shells down onto the ridge. At a given signal, the shelling stopped and foot soldiers from the 1st Brigade, followed by the 2nd and 3rd Brigades, charged at the Turkish positions. Charles Bean vividly described how 'the Australians rushed forward in the assault with the fury of fanatics, little heeding the tremendous shrapnel fire and enfilading rifle fire'.

Hoping to catch the enemy in disarray after the bombardment, the leading wave of Anzacs was stunned to find that the Turks had roofed their trenches with the logs they had cut from the local pines. 'None of the scouts had reported this in their nocturnal reconnaissance patrols,' notes historian Jonathan King. 'Unfazed, the Anzacs fired through gaps in the logs or tore them apart with their bare hands. They jumped into the trenches and shot or bayoneted the Turks in hand-to-hand fighting, hoping (but not always succeeding) not to shoot their own comrades in the dark caverns below.'

As is the way of war, the main point of the Lone Pine offensive was not so much to

capture the ridge itself but to divert the attention of the enemy from the main battle to the north, where New Zealand, British, Indian and Gurkha forces were being deployed to capture Chunuk Bair. It was a cruel twist that the diversionary attack succeeded in capturing the ridge, but the main battle was lost. Lone Pine Ridge was held by the Australian troops until the evacuation of the peninsula in December. Because so many Australian soldiers died with such gallantry near Lone Pine, it was chosen as the main Australian Anzac memorial site.

The horrors that the combatants endured at the height of the fighting are unimaginable today. Accounts written by some of the survivors record not just the carnage they suffered but the astonishing courage some men displayed despite it. Read this account, for example:

> Lone Pine was a battle of bombs, bullets and bayonets fought to defend sandbag walls built by both sides to block up a trench at the forward most point of the advance or counter attack. The Australians tried to hold what they had taken; the Turks fought equally determinedly to expel them from it.
>
> The action at one spot was typical of the fighting at Lone Pine. Lieutenant Frederick Tubb, 7th Battalion, of Longwood, Victoria, defended a position with eight men against a Turkish onslaught. As the enemy bombs fell upon them, Tubb told his men to smother them with Turkish greatcoats that lay about the trench. Some Turks broke through but were shot or bayoneted; others that tried to crawl in the open around the position were also killed. Tubb was everywhere, firing his revolver and leading by example. Slowly, men who were trying to catch and return bombs were being wounded. Corporal Frederick Wright, 7th Battalion, of Melbourne, clutched at a bomb that burst in his face killing him. Corporal Harry Webb, described by Bean as 'an orphan from Essendon', had both hands blown off, walked back out of the action and died. Bombs continued to burst and four more men were killed or wounded.
>
> Eventually, only Tubb, wounded in his arm and scalp, and two others, Corporals William Dunstan of Ballarat and Alexander Burton of Euroa, were left. A violent explosion blew down the Australian sandbag wall. Tubb drove the Turks back while Dunstan and Burton strove to rebuild the barrier when another bomb went off, killing Burton and blinding Dunstan. At that point reinforcements arrived, the position was saved and the Turks pulled back. When it was all over, Burton, Tubb and Dunstan, along with four other

Australians, were awarded Victoria Crosses for their outstanding courage at Lone Pine.

If you visit a war memorial today on Kirkland Street, Euroa, in Victoria, you'll find a granite archway at the main entrance, with a marble statue of a World War I soldier with arms reversed. Within the grounds are three fenced trees, planted in memory of Victoria Cross winners. Tubb and Burton lie there. Also in the park is an Aleppo pine – a descendant of the tree from Lone Pine – planted by the local Legacy group, with the simple inscription 'Lest We Forget'.

After the initial carnage at Lone Pine, eyewitnesses described dreadful scenes: The whole way across it is just one mass of dead bodies, bags of bombs, bales of sandbags, rifles, shovels and all the hundred and one things that had to be rushed across to the enemy trenches. The undergrowth has been cut down, like mown hay, simply stalks left standing, by the rifle fire, whilst the earth itself appears just as though one had taken a huge rake and scratched it all over. Here and there it is torn up where a shell has landed. Right beside me, within a space of fifteen feet, I can count fourteen of our boys stone dead. Ah! It is a piteous sight. Men and boys who yesterday were full of joy and life, now lying there, cold – cold – dead – their eyes glassy, their faces sallow and covered with dust – soulless – gone – somebody's son, somebody's boy – now merely a thing. Thank God that their loved ones cannot see them now – dead, with the blood congealed or oozing out. God, what a sight. The major is standing next to me and he says 'Well we have won'. Great God – won – that means victory and all those bodies within arm's reach – then may I never witness a defeat.

The pine tree that has come to physically represent the Anzac spirit of the place – the passion and the pain – has acquired a unique spiritual and memorial significance of its own. At numerous memorial sites across Australia today, you will find Aleppo pines of varying ages. Sceptics may doubt whether these trees have any special link with Gallipoli but they do have a strong claim to it. A number of versions circulate as to how the descendants of the Lone Pine Tree later came to be grown in Australia.

The Aleppo Pine in the grounds of the Australian War Memorial bears a plaque with the following inscription:

After the capture of the Lone Pine ridge in Gallipoli (6 August 1915), an

Australian soldier who had taken part in the attack, in which his brother was killed, found a cone on one of the branches used by the Turks as overhead cover for their trenches, and sent it to his mother. From seed shed by it she raised the tree, which she presented to be planted in the War Memorial grounds in honour of her own and others' sons who fell at Lone Pine.

In fact, history records that at least two Australian soldiers souvenired pinecones from the ridge and sent or brought them back to Australia. The soldier referred to in the War Memorial plaque was Lance Corporal Benjamin Smith of the 3rd Battalion, whose brother was killed in the battle for Lone Pine Ridge. Their mother Mrs McMullen who lived at Inverell, New South Wales, is said to have kept the cone for thirteen years before planting its seeds in 1928. Two grew into seedlings, one of which she presented to the town of Inverell and the other to the Parks and Gardens section of the Department of the Interior in Canberra. The Duke of Gloucester planted this second tree at the Australian War Memorial in October 1934. Today, it is more than twenty metres tall and in good condition.

Sergeant Keith McDowell, of the 24th Battalion, also souvenired a pinecone from Lone Pine. He is said to have carried the cone in his haversack until the war ended. On his return he gave it to an aunt, Mrs Emma Gray, who lived near Warrnambool in Victoria. Mrs Gray managed to raise four seedlings from it about ten years later. One was planted in May 1933 in Wattle Park, Melbourne, another at the Shrine of Remembrance in Melbourne, and another at the Soldiers Memorial Hall at The Sisters. The last was planted in the Warrnambool Gardens.

Since the 1980s, many trees have been grown by both seed and grafting techniques from material collected from the tree at the Australian War Memorial. These have been disseminated to many organisations including RSL branches and clubs, schools and other interested organisations. In 1990 two were taken back to be planted at Gallipoli by war veterans who attended the memorial service to mark the 75th anniversary of the battle of Lone Pine.

The Avenue of Honour

Sergeant J. Slade Hamilton sounded the trumpet on the Burrumbeet road, opposite the Ballarat Golf Course, at 3 o'clock on the boisterous, wet, cold June afternoon of the King's Birthday in 1917. Six trumpeters echoed his call down the road and 500 young Ballarat women started planting the trees in a long avenue which honours 3771 Ballarat men and nurses who went to the First World War. Twenty-five professional gardeners guided their hands and put in the stakes, and when the trumpets sounded again at 3.30, twenty-five professional carpenters attached name-plates to the stakes.

John Dargavel

Australia's involvement in World War I sparked an extraordinary outpouring of public fervour for memorials, and most of those grim marble and granite monuments in the main streets and parks of most large towns date from those times. More than 4000 have been documented and Australians are credited with having the highest number of war memorials per capita in the world. But the Great War also sparked great public interest in planting living memorials, in the form of groves and avenues of trees. For the first time in its young history, large numbers of Australians had died in an armed conflict. With such a small population, almost everyone knew a soldier who had served, been injured or died in the war. It was personal, and personal tributes seemed in order. Planting trees somehow fitted the bill. You could choose what type of tree to plant and where and why. Trees also had the virtue of life.

In all, more than 200 memorial avenues have been planted around Australia, honouring the memories of servicemen and women. It is a peculiarly Australian

phenomenon: no other nation responded to the war so vigorously. More than 120 of them were planted in the early 1900s, and Victorians accounted for 92 of them. They range from the victory avenue planted at Horsham for the South African war to a Vietnam avenue at Wodonga.

Australians have the most war memorials per capita in the world

Historian John Dargavel has made an extensive study of memorial avenues, especially in their strongholds of Victoria and Western Australia. In a richly detailed article on the issue – 'Trees Age and Memories Change in the Avenues of Honour and Remembrance' – Dargavel points out that unlike stone monuments, avenues of trees have three special attributes:

First is personal action: individual people could plant the trees that could be named for individual men or women, sometimes their relatives. Such a personal connection was hardly possible when a committee engaged a

In living memory

mason or builder to erect a monument. Second is the sense of a future which attaches to planting a small tree; a monument has only a past. Third is the natural dynamic of the tree's life which, like all living things, must age and die.

The ageing of the trees parallels how memories of war change and how mourning eases with time and fades over generations. Dargavel further says: 'Where monuments remain and remind, fading avenues allow us to forget.'

And forget we do. The subsequent fate of many memorial avenues is one of initial pride and nurturing, steady growth and slow decay. Some are brutalised by vandals, flattened by road-builders, die by fire or in drought, or simply perish because an inappropriate species was chosen for a poorly prepared site. The types of avenues we have planted have changed with time as well, especially in the choice of tree species, with a slow drift from exotic oaks, elms and pines of monumental stature to natives that give a more distinctly Australian vocabulary to the expression of grief.

To me, the most eloquent of them all is the extraordinary avenue of 2500 trees planted by one man, J.L.F. 'Fen' Woodburn, beside the Goulburn Valley Highway near Shepparton, in memory of his son. It consists of a double row of eucalypts – including river red gums, lemon-scented gums, yellow gum, spotted gum, honey box and red ironbark – on either side of the highway. Calder Woodburn was killed in France in 1942 while serving with the Royal Australian Air Force. His grieving father planted the trees between 1943 and 1949; in time he decided to dedicate the avenue to all servicemen from the district who did not return from the war. Memorial name plates were fixed to 110 of the trees, in each case to the tree nearest to the home of the dead man. Most of the trees remain alive and well today and the Calder Woodburn Memorial Avenue of Honour stretches for almost twenty kilometres. It is the largest memorial of its kind dating from World War II and is exceptional for its use of only eucalypt species. This unique memorial was added to the National Trust of Australia (Victoria) Register of Significant Trees in 1988 and the Australian Heritage Commission Register of the National Estate in 1992. Over time, self-seeded and invasive tree species had begun to intrude on the avenue's appearance, so a conservation management plan was developed in 2001 – by government and community interests – and Victorian Heritage Program funds were used to give the avenue a facelift in 2005.

But why were Victorians so passionate about memorial avenues when most other states weren't? There's little doubt the answer lies in the greatest memorial avenue of them all, at Ballarat. It was one of the earliest and largest avenues of its kind and one of the most complete to have survived the passage of time. The sheer enthusiasm with which the people of Ballarat approached the task seems to have been the spark that ignited so much interest elsewhere in Victoria. With the Ballarat memorial, military rank was not a key consideration: a soldier was a soldier, and a tree was a tree. What mattered most was that every sacrifice made in the national interest was given equal weight and acknowledgment. The result is a living tribute of monumental scale along a major road in an otherwise fairly bland landscape.

The idea for the avenue began with Mrs Tilly Thompson, a charismatic director of a local fashion clothing manufacturer, E. Lucas & Co. The idea clearly clicked in a big way with the employees and the community. In the two years to August 1919, exactly 3771 mainly exotic trees were planted along 22 kilometres of the Western Highway, one for each soldier who enlisted as a resident of the urban area of Ballarat. The trees were planted, with tree-guards and memorial plaques placed in order of the soldier's enlistment. The Prince of Wales performed the official opening. The 500 'Lucas Girls' had not only raised the money required, but gave up their weekends to plant the trees.

The avenue still offers a memorable green gateway into the City of Ballarat, and is located along the Ballarat Burrumbeet Road (the former Western Highway) about four kilometres north-west of the city centre. It now consists of 3332 trees: it begins at the Arch of Victory in Alfredton, runs west to Lake Burrumbeet, where it changes direction and heads north, crossing the Western Freeway Bypass and continuing along Avenue Road to Weatherboard Learmonth Road. It is a continuous avenue except where the Western Freeway Bypass has been built across it. The species planted were American ash, English ash, mountain ash, North American maple, scarlet oak, Norway maple, broadleaf maple, English maple, alder, lime, Ontario poplar, silver birch, deciduous cypress, sailors oak, purple-leaf elm, new silver poplar, tulip tree, Huntingdon elm, Canadian giant elms, oriental plane, black Italian poplar, sugar maple and chestnut oak. Individual species were usually planted in blocks of about 50 trees. By 1934 most of the original Avenue name plates fixed to the tree guards were lost or missing and were replaced with permanent bronze name plaques with no reference to title or rank: a cross below a soldier's name indicates that he was one of the 529 killed in action. An Arch of Victory was added later, again courtesy of the fundraising efforts of the Lucas Girls. When the arch was officially opened in 1921 they presented the prince with a handmade pair of satin-charmeuse pyjamas – embroidered with sprigs of wattle and three kookaburras on a gum tree branch.

That early enthusiasm for avenues of honour waned as Australian society and the nature of war changed. As Dargavel points out, by World War II:

Empire fervour did not cut as much ice in 1939 – the horrors of the Western Front had seen to that – but it was still assumed that Britain's war was Australia's too. . . . There were powerful social changes so that the Australia of 1945 was a very different country from that in which the Lucas Girls had started planting their avenue in 1917. Their daughters were more likely to be in a munitions factory, or working on a farm, or in the forces themselves than their mothers; and they waved to the GIs arriving as much as at the local lads departing. And when the war ended, they were caught up in the general rush to reconstruct the country in a confident and more independent way.

Australians thought of this war in a different way and wanted to commemorate it differently, too: conscripts weren't volunteers, Dunkirk was not Gallipoli, and the genocide of the Jews and the horrors of Hiroshima loomed much larger on the scale of grief. 'Stone monuments, so typical of World War I, were not required, or so most people felt, preferring that memorials, if any, should have a socially useful purpose,' says Dargavel. 'Hospitals, halls, parks, swimming pools and schools were favoured and it was found sufficient in most places to add new names to old monuments.' But new trees were added to some of the old Avenues of Honour – those that had not died meanwhile – and Australian natives came more into favour: red flowering gum at Drouin, mahogany gums at Puckapunyal, sugar gums at Pyramid Hill and casuarinas and sugar gums at Kings Park in Western Australia.

It would be nice to think that these trees will inspire generations to come with a respect for life and an abhorrence of war. If nothing else, let's hope they serve the purpose for which they were planted: to help us remember personal sacrifice and to let us forget personal grief.

Facing page:
A memorable gateway
to the City of Ballarat

The Soldiers Walk

HOBART, TASMANIA

The story of the rise, fall and rise of the Soldiers Walk memorial avenue in the Queens Domain, Hobart, is as uplifting as it is sad. Inspired by the Ballarat memorial, Hobart's returned soldiers joined with citizens and public officials to acquire and plant 520 trees in 1918 and 1919, in memory of mainly local men who died in service during World War I. First known as the Soldiers Memorial Avenue, it was renamed in the 1980s as the Soldiers Walk. Like most plantings of the day, exotic species were chosen – mainly cedars and cypress. Large crowds had turned out to prepare the ground before planting began. Each seedling was surrounded by a tree-guard and carried a board naming a dead soldier.

The first planting day in August 1918 generated massive public support. The local newspaper reported:

All creeds and classes, sharing the same sorrows, and bound together by the same deep-set bonds of love and nationality as weld their heroic sons were represented. Mothers and fathers in mourning for loved ones resting on lonely hillsides at Gallipoli and the rural cemeteries of France had healing wounds reopened … At every tree there were touching incidents. At one, returned men filled the earth in memory of a 'digger' who had nobody here to do it for him, no friends but the friends of his dugout and the trenches. At Lieut. Hare's tree, his tiny mite of a nephew, four months old, assisted by his uncle, heaped the earth round it while his soldier uncles and many friends who knew him well in Hobart looked on. Feeble old ladies and gentlemen, hand in hand attended to others, and with the 429 trees planted were the same sorrowful scenes.

At the second planting day in 1919, Governor and Lady Newdegate each planted a seedling – he an oak from Gallipoli and she 'a laurel from the Forum in Rome'. As the *Mercury* reported, Lord Newdegate gave a thoughtful speech:

> It is easy to put up monuments of stone to their memory, and we are glad to do so, but I think the idea of planting trees, which, as the years go on, will grow and increase, is splendid, because when people come and walk along your beautiful domain they will see those trees growing, and will always be reminded that they were planted in memory of those who, without fear, had gone and done what they considered their duty. The sympathy of all us goes to the families who have lost members in this war. I think it must be a source of pride to them to think that they are able in the neighbourhood of the city from which many of these gallant men enlisted, to plant trees which they will be able to look after always, and which will stand as a memorial to those men who have gone. I feel very grateful to a friend of mine in Victoria, Mr Winter Cook, who has given me this little oak tree which you see here. It was brought by a nephew of his who has Tasmanian blood in his veins – Captain Cook a member of the Victorian army – as an acorn from the Gallipoli peninsula, a small corner of the world which will always be remembered in history as the place where the gallant men of your 1st Division did such stirring deeds. This little tree actually comes from an acorn that grew on the peninsula and here it is planted in your beautiful domain. I am sure it will be a labour of love with the people of Hobart to see that the trees are properly looked after. I think and hope it will be of interest to you to have this little tree actually springing from an acorn, which came from that place, which has given us such glorious history.

Like most other memorials of its kind, this one at first thrived and was lovingly cared for. As relatives and friends of the dead moved away, grew old or died, the avenue fell gradually into disrepair, despite occasional bursts of fresh interest. The original name boards and tree-guards slowly perished and were removed and trees that died were replaced at times with species unsympathetic to the visual appeal of the avenue, including Tasmanian blue gums. In 1960, some 80 trees were bulldozed to make way for a rubbish tip that evolved into a sporting field. Over time, other parts were used for temporary car parking, the nameplates were removed, and some trees were scorched by fires fuelled in part by invasive weeds and native plants. But in 2002 a group of local

In living memory

residents and descendants of the dead rallied to halt the avenue's sad decline. Out of a public meeting, the group Friends of Soldiers Walk was formally incorporated, with an impressive website, <http://www.soldierswalk.org.au>, the source of much of the information here. It has more than 200 members and supporters and links to many descendants of soldiers of the Walk. In an odd twist of fate – or an appropriate one, depending on your point of view – the group notes that the site is home to some rare and endangered indigenous plants. They grow protected from invasive grasses that have been shaded out by larger trees, 'thus the most exotic protects the rarest natives'.

Proclamation,
Separation,
Federation

Tree ceremonies

All Australian settlements, large and small, began out of necessity with the cutting down of trees. They were the raw material from which our towns and cities were built, and their removal was effected with little sentiment and mostly without commemoration. It wasn't long, however, before planting a tree took on a specific ceremonial role to mark significant events. For a new nation, planting trees symbolised an intention to grow and endure, an act of self-belief and of faith in the future.

The species of tree and the dignitaries chosen to plant them were also symbols of older cultural links with distant lands. There are many royal trees, for example, dotted around the country as reminders of visits by reigning or future British monarchs, their vice-regal representatives or members of the various royal families. Mainly exotic trees were planted – oaks, elms and pines were favoured – but natives occasionally got the nod as well.

The visit of Prince Alfred, then Duke of Edinburgh, to Australia in 1868 resulted in one of the most prolific flurries of royal tree plantings. Not all the locals were happy about it: one seedling he planted in Sydney's Parramatta Park was subsequently torn from the ground and hacked to pieces. Another tree, a Norfolk pine, was planted at the Sydney harbourside suburb of Clontarf in remembrance of a more significant event that occurred there during his visit.

While the Duke was enjoying a picnic, an Irishman named Henry James O'Farrell shot him in the back with a pistol. It was Australia's first attempted political assassination. Large angry crowds gathered in Sydney, and anti-Irish sentiment ran high. Butler Aspinall, who had appeared for some of the Eureka Stockade defendants, later represented O'Farrell in court. The Duke's injuries were minor – the bullet bounced off his ribs – and he soon recovered, but his would-be assassin was quickly convicted and hanged for his crime. The commemorative tree at Clontarf grew very large and in modern times has had a nearby plaque that reads:

This tree marks the spot where an attempt was made to assassinate H.R.H. the Duke of Edinburgh (son of Her Majesty Queen Victoria) while he was attending the picnic of the Sailors' Home on March 12, 1868. This tablet replaces one erected in 1930 by the Manly Municipal Council in conjunction with the Manly Warringah and Pittwater Historical Society.

That's just one of many colourful stories trees tell of our past, none more so than those that mark our beginnings.

115

The Old Gum Tree

GLENELG, SOUTH AUSTRALIA

The first British settlers came ashore nervously in November 1836 from three ships anchored at Holdfast Bay, in St Vincent's Gulf, South Australia. They had sailed half-way across the world chasing a dream of a new life in a country they knew nothing about and in a settlement that did not yet exist.

About a kilometre inland, they pitched tents and built temporary huts. For his tent, Robert Gouger, the Colonial Secretary, chose a site shaded by large gum trees, one of them with its trunk bent over bizarrely in the shape of an arch. To its trunk and branches he attached his tent ropes, to give his flimsy official residence a little more solidity.

The settlers found themselves in a beautiful natural setting, with freshwater lagoons teeming with ducks and other water fowl and the surrounding tufts of kangaroo grass sheltering abundant quail. The shrieks of cockatoos and the squawking of brightly coloured parrots filled the air by day. But by night squadrons of hungry mosquitoes sucked their blood and drove some to distraction. Enormous stinging ants and blinking frogs invaded their tents. At one point, a weary Gouger lay on his couch and dropped his hand to the sandy soil below, but recoiled in horror when he realised his fingers were only centimetres from a scorpion.

Expectations were high: the Surveyor General William Light was busy scouting out the best site for the beautiful city he was preparing to lay out, inspired by the garden-city movement of the day; this was to be a fully planned, self-contained community with designated areas for homes, offices, shops, industry and farms. Still, Christmas Day was a time of some reflection and a sense of loss for the familiar Yuletide rituals of England. In place of snow, carols, turkey and the comforts of their religion, they had

An odd tree that marked the birth of South Australia

insects, searing heat, parrot pie and not even the semblance of a church, let alone an ordained man of the cloth. But big changes were coming.

A few days later, a survey party spotted a large ship sailing up St Vincent Gulf. It was the *Buffalo*, with the vice-regal party headed by John Hindmarsh and more emigrants. The newcomers anchored in Holdfast Bay on 28 December for a heart-sinking night. The midsummer heat was appalling and massive bushfires were raging on the Mount Lofty ranges, the reflected light so bright that those on board the *Buffalo* could make out the people on board their sister ship, the *Cygnet*, sailing almost a kilometre away.

In the morning, a boat was sent ashore to fetch Gouger and the Deputy Surveyor General, George Kingston, to confer with Hindmarsh. William Light was inland at the time, standing atop a hill commanding a view of the plains by the River Torrens where he thought he had found the best site for the future city of Adelaide. The Governor's party came ashore at 2 pm in three boats, with the colony's new Chaplain, the Treasurer and others, and twenty uniformed marines. The officials gathered in the shade of the bent tree.

A brief handwritten statement by Hindmarsh was read aloud by his secretary, George Stevenson:

> Proclamation by His Excellency John Hindmarsh, Knight of the Royal Hanoverian Order Governor and Commander in Chief of the Province of South Australia, in announcing to the colonists of His Majesty's Province of South Australia, the establishment of the Government, I hereby call upon them to conduct themselves on all occasions with order and quietness, duly to respect the laws, and by a course of industry and sobriety, by a practice of sound morality and a strict observance of the ordinances of religion, to prove themselves worthy to be the Founders of a great and free colony.

The same protection as 'the rest of His Majesty's subjects' was to be accorded to 'the native inhabitants', who were 'to be considered as much under the safeguard of the law as the colonists themselves, and equally entitled to the privileges of British subjects'.

With those noble sentiments and words of command, British law and Government were now firmly in place. The province of South Australia had been born, a brave new experiment in planned, free settlement, without convict labour. The temperature was a withering 114° F (45° C); even in the shade of the tree it was still 100° F. It wasn't conducive to much activity, but those present did manage to toast their success and dine on a 'cold collation' including dressed Hampshire ham. We can only imagine the clammy discomfort of the ladies in their long dresses and the men in their itchy regalia. The marines fired a volley into the air, the white ensign was hoisted and the ships in the bay fired a salute from their guns. An official draft of the proclamation was then taken to be printed on a cast-iron manual Stanhope Press set up nearby in a reed hut.

With the formalities concluded, the official party returned to the *Buffalo*. Those left behind got on with the informal celebrations, with the help of more than a little alcohol. 'While the sailors became intoxicated and the natives were setting fire to the woods, the last of the colonists to arrive were unable to conceal their disappointment with the outcome of their hazardous 158-day voyage,' local historian Dulcie Perry wrote. 'They had expected to occupy the land they had purchased long before they left England.'

Every year since, the same Proclamation has been read out publicly on the anniversary of that day, with the Governor, Premier and Mayor of the City of Holdfast Bay leading the official ceremony. The actual proclamation site is now a small well-kept reserve in McFarlane Street, North Glenelg, surrounded by a typical beachside suburb. Yet it still has as its centrepiece the Old Gum Tree by which that first ceremony took place. The tree is long dead, but the bulk of its bizarre trunk is sheltered from the worst of the elements by a large purpose-built canopy and what appears to be a generous filling of concrete to hold together its greyed decaying wood (not the best preservation treatment). It is an odd and memorable tree that grew sideways, its trunk snaking up and down as if it had tried and failed to grow upright. In profile it looks a little like the fabled Loch Ness monster.

As the Old Gum Tree gradually aged and died, South Australia grew and prospered and, after a faltering start, did achieve some of its loftier goals of being a great and free colony. It was not able to honour Hindmarsh's noble words in defence of the rights of Adelaide's Aborigines, because their society and way of life was soon dislocated and all but destroyed. But South Australia did pioneer the rights of women. It granted voting rights in local government elections to female property owners as early as 1861. The passing of the 1856 Constitution Act was the most advanced democratic constitution in the world at that time, bringing in the principle of one man–one vote and secret ballots. All adult women won the right to vote in 1895, second only to those enfranchised in New Zealand two years earlier, and the South Australian Parliament was the first to allow women to be elected members. The Pitjantjatjara Land Rights Act in 1981 also extended the principle of indigenous land rights in advance of any other state.

Paradoxically, given the ongoing respect accorded to the Old Gum Tree over the past 170 years, South Australia has a sorry record of tree-clearing. It is the driest state in the driest inhabited continent: that, coupled with the extensive and sometimes reckless land clearances for agriculture in the past, makes it now also the state with the least tree cover. About 80 per cent of all the land that gets enough rain to make it suitable for agriculture – and thus for woodlands and forests – was cleared by 1985.

But attitudes change and Adelaide, at least, is now the 'greenest' of Australia's capital cities in the sense that it has more trees lining its streets and roadways than any other. As well, in 2002 the city adopted a five-year, $10 million urban forest program that will see an extra million trees planted – one for every human inhabitant of the city. That plan is designed to promote environmental as well as social benefits and, in time, will join up with a grander revegetation program that will link new and remnant bush plantings with trees, understorey plants and native grasses to foster wildlife and biodiversity. The Old Gum Tree may yet take on a new symbolic significance, not just as an emblem of the city's history but as a reminder of the need to conserve and reclaim its lost natural heritage as well.

The Old Gum Tree is one of the few heritage trees where serious effort has been made for visitors

Preservation

The Old Gum Tree is one of the few historic trees in Australia that has had serious efforts made to display it and to provide high-quality interpretive signage explaining its significance for visitors. The park surrounding it is neatly gardened and there's a homely, friendly atmosphere about the whole scene.

The stump of the so-called Explorer's Tree in the Blue Mountains, west of Sydney, was also filled with concrete at one point – to remedy termite damage – but chemical reactions hastened its demise. As a supposed monument to the blazing of a route across the mountains from Sydney by Blaxland, Wentworth and Lawson in 1813, that stump is a pathetically inadequate wreck. Indeed, it is a model of how not to preserve an historic tree. After it died decades ago, it was hacked back to a stump and the bulk of it taken elsewhere as a curiosity display and was consumed by a bushfire. When I last visited the stump it was roofed but still largely exposed to the open air and to souvenir hunters, despite its advanced age and severe state of decay. A busy highway whistles past, visitor access is poor, and the explanatory signage is minimal. It has long been poorly maintained and is garishly lit at night.

Its crumbling wood is only held together with steel straps and some mindless vandal recently tried to set fire to it. To top it all off, the tree itself is unlikely even to have been an authentic relic of the trio's journey: it is beyond coincidence that it is not mentioned in their journals, nor by other early explorers, nor by the roadbuilder William Cox, nor even by Governor Macquarie, who in 1815 visited and named the very hill on which it stands.

The Proclamation Tree

PERTH, WESTERN AUSTRALIA

On 12 August 1829, the King's birthday, Mrs Helena Dance ceremonially performed the first formal act to mark the birth of what has become the thriving city of Perth. Mrs Dance was the wife of the commander of HMS *Sulphur*, the ship that had brought the first European settlers to the continent's west coast. She was watched by a small group of colonists, dignitaries, troops and officials.

Mrs Dance stood a sandy ridge fronting the Swan River, in a scene of much beauty and tranquillity. Ducks and black swans swam on the reed-lined river, dotted about were the mop-tops of ancient grass trees and nearby were tall stands of eucalypt forest and wildflowers. At the given signal, Mrs Dance lifted an axe and sank its blade into the trunk of a casuarina tree. It was duly felled and the Swan River Colony was on its way.

Speeches were made, celebratory shots rang out and those assembled cheered when it was announced that the town to be built here would be named Perth, after the birthplace of Sir George Murray, then British Secretary for the Colonies. As historian Ruth Marchant-James points out, two months later a visitor who strolled through the modest township noted that the proposed main street:

> … was at present, only adorned with lofty trees and a variety of lovely flowers. In my perambulations, I fell in with the written newspaper of the place, appended to a stately eucalyptus tree, where among other public notices, I observed the Governor's permission for one individual to practice as a notary, another as a surgeon, and a third as an auctioneer.

Foundation Tree

Exactly where Mrs Dance's casuarina – Perth's Foundation Tree – was cut down is not known, although a plaque set into the footpath near the corner of Barrack and Hay streets commemorates its demise. But you can still see a piece of the actual tree in the form of a small sewing box made from its wood, held in the Western Australian Museum's collections. The highly polished box has brass hinges, nine inner compartments and is lined with blue velvet. It was made – probably in England – for Mrs Ellen Stirling, wife of the colony's early lieutenant governor, but was lost to history until 1932, when in a remarkable coincidence Queen Mary came across it in a London curiosity shop. The Queen knew her antiques and recognised its significance: she bought it and presented it as a gift to the Western Australian Government. It has a small brass plaque on its lid that reads: 'This box was made from the tree which was cut down at Swan River in 1829 by His Excellency James Stirling for the purpose of laying the foundation of the Capital of Western Australia.' It is a mystery why Mrs Dance's name was replaced by Stirling's, but history records that is was she who swung the axe.

Another historic tree linked to Perth's constitutional history is the splendid Moreton Bay fig known as the Proclamation Tree. It was planted by the colony's first governor, Sir William Robinson, on 21 October 1890 to commemorate the adoption of Western Australia's new Constitution, which came into force that day and gave the colony responsible self-government. It still stands at the junction of Queen Victoria, Adelaide and Parry streets, in the busy centre of the port of Fremantle. The press reported the occasion:

> The Mayor requested His Excellency to plant the tree in commemoration of the great boon, which had been conferred on the colony. His Excellency having expressed his pleasure in complying, planted the tree using a gilded spade. This function over, the Mayor specially requested Sir William to address those present, reminding him that many had not heard him speak. His Excellency graciously complied. He said that, having spoken so much since his arrival, he would not do more than express his hope that the tree just planted would flourish, and that its growth and size would be symbolical of the growth and magnitude of the free institutions and prosperity in store for the colony.

In keeping with the fashion of the day, Moreton Bay figs were often chosen for their majestic proportions for landscaping and memorial plantings, even though they were native to the east coast. Phillip Webster, a Fremantle auditor, provided the Proclamation Tree. Webster was a tree-lover who planted many of the old trees visible today around Fremantle. They include some at St John's Church, in King's Square. On Proclamation Day in 1930, young students from Fremantle Boys School donated and erected a plaque by the tree acknowledging its significance. For the 1996 anniversary, the plaque was restored and unveiled, and the Governor General, Michael Jeffery, read the proclamation. Witnessing these events were twenty of the very students – now old men – who had provided the plaque all those years earlier.

The Federal Oak

MELBOURNE, VICTORIA

A recurring motif in the red and green carpets throughout Melbourne's grand old Parliament House is an oak-leaf pattern. Although it's unclear exactly why Victoria's legislative house has decorative links with a British tree and not a locally indigenous one, it is said that the pattern represents the oak tree under which the Magna Carta was signed, and as such is a symbol of freedom and liberty. But the Parliament does have a rather special living oak in the Parliamentary Gardens that is of wider significance to all Australians. Known as the Federal Oak, it was planted in 1890 by Sir Henry Parkes to mark the start of the Australasian Federal Convention, when representatives of the six colonies met to map out the road to a central national government. It was to be eleven more years before a seemingly interminable jumble of inter-colony rivalry and feuding – with argument and counter-argument on everything from defence and quarantine to taxes and railway gauges – was finally resolved and Australia became united and self-governing. Many commemorative saplings were planted to mark the occasion, but the Federal Oak – by that time a flourishing young tree – has the honour of officially being the first.

The Parliamentary Oaks

CANBERRA, AUSTRALIAN CAPITAL TERRITORY

On 9 May 1927, more than 30 000 proud Australians gathered outside the brand new stark-white Parliament House in Canberra for its official opening by the Duke of York. Dame Nellie Melba trilled a welcome to the Duke and Duchess with a rendition of 'God Save the King' and, as historian Manning Clark noted: 'From the steps the Duke urged the people to listen to the voices of the noble army of the dead and march in step with them towards a glorious destiny.'

To mark this momentous event, the Duke planted a young English oak tree the following day on the corner of State Circle and Kings Avenue in Barton, just 500 metres from where the new Parliament House stands today. After careful planning, the oak had been brought to Australia as a live tree from the Royal Botanic Gardens in Kew, London, to literally put down the roots of the Westminster system in Australian soil. In deference to post-colonial sensibilities, at the same ceremony the Duke also planted an Australian bunya pine across Kings Avenue. The fact that he did so was significant. The Chief Commissioner of the Federal Capital Commission, J.H. Butters – backed by Prime Minister Stanley Bruce – came up with the idea for dual English–Australian ceremonial tree plantings specifically for this occasion. The policy continued at least until 1949, when the first tree plantings were carried out at what is now the Australian National Botanic Gardens, when Prime Minister Ben Chifley planted an English oak and the Director of Kew Gardens, Lord Salisbury, planted a white spotted gum.

The rest of the Canberra parliamentary plantation was added later, with another 77 English oak trees being planted, possibly as an unemployment relief project. There were plans for six others around the national capital but the Barton oak grove is the only one of all those commemorative plantings that remains largely intact today: the fate of some remains a mystery and others are reduced to remnants. The heritage significance of the plantation meant that it was placed on the Register of the National Estate in 1997. It is also on the Commonwealth Heritage List.

The oaks were planted in six rows of thirteen trees each, evenly spaced twelve metres apart. The ground was not cultivated beforehand, so native grasses were allowed to remain growing around the holes dug for the seedlings. The 74 trees that remain alive are mature and healthy. They have grown up to fifteen metres high and some have crowns spreading up to twenty metres, according to Dr Robert Boden, a former director of the Australian National Botanic Gardens and a tree expert who takes a close interest in the plantation. The bunya pine, incidentally, is thriving and each year produces the thumping great seed cones for which the species is both famous and infamous (you don't want one falling on you).

With their crowns now touching, in time the oaks could develop a shady mini-ecosystem in their own right. Another oak in the Australian Capital Territory is known to be 150 years old, Boden points out. Since oaks can live for centuries, there's every reason to believe that this highly significant stand of trees may indeed fulfil the sentiment expressed by the Duke of York and have a long and glorious destiny – a truly fitting memorial to the founding of the national parliament.

Yet by 2004, the future of the plantation was under such threat that the National Trust of Australia felt compelled to put it on its Endangered Places list. Little maintenance was being done, invasive native and exotic weed species infested parts of it, some of the trees on one side were stressed by cars being parked underneath them and few people found it inviting enough to use for recreation. To top it off, the Federal Department of Finance and Administration saw the prestigious York Park North land as a 'prime office site' and proposed to allow a multistorey building and car park to be built there. Calling for an immediate care and maintenance program to be implemented for the trees, the Trust's listing notes said:

> The formality evident in the plantation has created a landscape with substantial historic significance. The formal arrangement of the oak plantation, and the use of a large number of a single species in wide spacing are unusual. There are six rows of trees, each originally of thirteen trees. While several trees have been removed and two dead trees remain in situ, the plantation remains largely as originally conceived . . . Of immediate concern, is the stressed condition of the plantation, reflecting a long period of neglect by the Commonwealth authorities.

At the time of writing, the plantation's future was still unclear, despite claims to the contrary by public officials and politicians. Robert Boden told me that a temporary fence had been installed to deter car parking beneath some of the trees, but the only other maintenance he was aware of in the previous year was that the grass and weeds beneath the trees had been mown. A draft conservation plan even allowed for the possibility of office buildings being erected within the plantation itself and for about 30 of these 80-year-old trees to be removed and transplanted elsewhere. It is puzzling that such a large and venerable memorial – sitting right under the noses of the nation's most senior officials and public representatives – could go neglected and inadequately protected. It does not speak well of our collective sense of respect either for our cultural roots or for our heritage trees generally: if trees that mark an event of undoubted national significance have an uncertain future, what hope is there for all the other trees – great and small – that tell Australia's story?

The Separation Tree

MELBOURNE, VICTORIA

They hooped, hollered, hurrahed, lit bonfires and partied as never before: after a decade of concerted lobbying and campaigning, Melbourne was finally free to cast off the despised administrative shackles of Sydney. On the evening of 11 November 1850, word came through from Adelaide – the gateway of news carried by ships from England – that the British Parliament had agreed finally to separate the Port Phillip District from New South Wales. Melburnians were delirious: Victoria was to be self-governing. Until then, they had a mere six representatives in the 36-member New South Wales Legislative Council. Sydney didn't just control political power but took an unreasonably large slice of the district's economic pie as well, and Melbourne keenly wanted both back for itself. It had never felt an integral part of the first colony: it was free of the stain of convicts, and was settled first from Tasmania and built by direct immigration from Britain. Melbourne was growing and, by population size and economy, was becoming a serious rival to Sydney. Now it would be able to steer its own course and the future fairly glowed with optimism and hope.

Officially, a public holiday was declared. Unofficially, the festivities went on for months. By the time the formalities were completed and the actual split took place on 1 July 1851, Separation Day itself was a bit of a fizzer. The discovery of gold just a week later quickly overwhelmed public interest. Separation Day, however, was vigorously celebrated for many years afterwards, until other commemorative days took on more significance. One memorial to that happy time that has endured steadily ever since is, of course, a tree.

As the news spread, a General Rejoicings Committee was formed. Dinners and balls were held; beacons were set alight and firework displays lit the night sky;

Still thriving: the Separation Tree where Victorians celebrated in 1850

The Separation Tree

Without doubt, the long and rich human story associated with the Separation Tree makes it one of Australia's greatest trees. It even carries a record of environmental history in the form of a large iron spike that was driven into it in 1891 – and remains visible today – to mark the height reached by the Yarra's waters during a great flood. Soon after, the Yarra was realigned. Although the Separation Tree survived that change, many other red gums and trees of Australia's riverbanks and wetlands have suffered greatly from human re-engineering of watercourses, dam-building, water extraction and flood-mitigation measures.

So it was intriguing and appropriate that in late 2005, the Separation Tree was enlisted into a new symbolic role, as an urban ambassador for its rural cousins. Mildura's celebrity chef Stefano de Pieri, a passionate champion of the Murray River, stood beneath it to launch a new campaign by conservationists to protect the river's endangered red gum forests:

> Seventy-five per cent of the red gums on the Murray River are dead or dying but state governments are allowing logging and grazing to further degrade them, threatening endangered species such as the superb parrot. The biggest red gum wetland forest in the world, the Barmah Millewa Forest is still being logged and grazed. Places like this should be National Parks and be jointly managed by traditional owners. Can you imagine a more serene moment than cooking up a Murray cod, under a cathedral of 400-year-old red gums, as the Murray River flows by?

It's not just the Barmah Forest red gums that are in trouble: millions of others face an uncertain future without better water-management policies and practices. Many have already died of neglect, starved of water for agriculture. How fitting that the publicity campaign in which the Separation Tree stars is a joint cross-border initiative of environmentalists from Victoria and New South Wales. They are calling on governments of both states to come together to better manage the red gum forests on their mutual border. It's a nice thought that this symbol of their partition might reunite Victoria and New South Wales for the common good of such valuable trees. That would be something to hoop and holler about, all over again.

balloons carrying slips of paper announcing the Separation were released. On 15 November, a new bridge across the Yarra River was to be opened and people came from everywhere to celebrate. A newspaper correspondent writing under the name Garryowen reported:

> Never before or since had there been a sight of such revel in Melbourne, considering the population and circumstances. There was a classified procession of over a mile long, celebrating on the way, the opening of the new Prince's Bridge, the aggregation of all being 5000 or 6000 individuals, with many school children. The bridge having been opened by Mr La Trobe, the whole concourse entered the Government Domain and the Botanic Gardens, where the children's picnic also took place …

Other reports put the crowd at more than 20000. The procession was 'led by the Saxe Horn band of Mr Hore and with members of societies and lodges carrying banners'. The children were said to have consumed some 10000 buns.

During and after the Gardens picnic 'a considerable meeting of citizens gathered under, as well as about, the large gum tree . . . celebrating the event of the granting of the colonists' prayer by the Home Government in a happy and creditable fashion'.

The tree in question was already a much-admired river red gum, and today it occupies a special place in Melbourne's heart. Visit the Royal Botanic Gardens now and you should find it alive and reasonably well despite the passing of more than 150 years. Indeed, it looks in better shape now than it did in some old photographs, like the one in the Victorian archives taken in 1906 which shows it looking decidedly worse for wear with foliage missing and dead branches in its crown.

It is an impressive red gum by any standards, with a chest-high trunk diameter close to 1.5 metres, a height of about 28 metres and a foliage spread of more than twenty metres (in 1915, 30 years after a number of large decayed limbs were pruned, it was measured as having a trunk about one metre in diameter and a height of about twenty metres). Its crown is supported by a handful of sturdy limbs but it was a little threadbare of leaves when I last visited it in late summer. The trunk was fitted with a large clear-plastic collar, as are many other trees in the Gardens, to deter the ubiquitous possums from climbing it to feast on young shoots. Dark flaky bark clings to the lower trunk and gradually thins to leave the upper branches pale and bare. All in all, the old tree is doing fine in its twilight years, under the circumstances.

Equally impressive – if not more so – is a truly ancient red gum nearby on the edge of the Ornamental Lake: it is another of the few survivors that can unquestionably claim to be original inhabitants of inner Melbourne. It sprang up on the Lower Yarra River long before the lake was constructed from a shallow lagoon in the 1890s, when a bank was built to control its regular flooding. The old tree does not appear to have suffered much as a result. It is a splendid beast, craggy and majestic, complete with all manner of lumps, bumps, burls, hollows and amputations that tell a life story we can only imagine. It is known as the Lion's Head Tree for the enormous woody callus that wells out from its lower trunk. If you go there, be sure to pay it your respects: stand with it a while and you'll be well rewarded.

Trees – often exotic – marked the visit of many a dignitary

THIS OAK
WAS PLANTED BY
HER EXCELLENCY LADY DENMAN
ON THE 12th APRIL, 1913
TO COMMEMORATE THE VISIT
TO FERNSHAW
ON THE 15th MAY, 1901 OF
HER MAJESTY QUEEN MARY
THEN DUCHESS OF YORK
CONSORT OF HIS MOST GRACIOUS MAJESTY
KING GEORGE THE FIFTH
Her Majesty Lunched Close To This Spot
The Acorn From Which The Oak Was Grown
Was Sent To Melbourne From The
Royal Gardens Windsor Castle

At the base of the Separation Tree is a plaque unveiled in 1951 by the Governor, Sir Dallas Brooks, to commemorate the centenary of Separation Day. Close by on a lawn above it there's another river red gum planted on that centenary day, a sapling grown from the Separation Tree's seed. It is intended as a replacement for the parent tree in the event of its death. Far too few of our historic trees have had the benefit of such an insurance policy: if it's good enough for rare species, why not historic individuals? So far, the policy doesn't look like being needed any time soon and, in the meantime, Separation Tree Junior has grown to impressive proportions. Although it is slimmer and has a smaller foliage spread, it had already exceeded 30 metres in height when it was measured in 1993.

No one knows exactly how old the Separation Tree is, but it was clearly already a handsome and mature tree in 1851. It may well be more than three centuries old. Unconfirmed historical reports suggest that it was a gathering place for Aborigines before white settlement: if so, it must have been a substantial tree at the time. It was certainly singled out for keeping when the Gardens were first being developed, with mention of it being a fine red gum with widespread branches.

An early deputy director of the Gardens, Ambrose Neate, followed the tree's progress with special interest and affection for many years. His archived notebooks recall that when he joined the Gardens in a junior office role in 1858, at the age of fifteen, the tree was 'in its prime', and its central position on a lawn made it a favourite for shading picnics. Neate made reference to assertions that the actual opening of the Gardens took place beneath the tree. Charles La Trobe, the former Superintendent of the Port Phillip District, newly elevated to the position of Lieutenant Governor of Victoria, is also said to have read the proclamation declaration under the tree on the first Separation Day. Even if he did not, there was certainly a significant public gathering at the tree on that day, which carried a formal resolution of congratulations to Queen Victoria for her proclamation. A commemorative plaque, no longer in place, read: 'Under this tree on 15th November 1850 public rejoicings of citizens of Melbourne took place in celebration of the authorised separation of the Colony of Victoria from New South Wales on 1st July 1851.' Curiously, in view of the public sentiment for the Separation Tree, La Trobe planted an English elm nearby to mark the occasion. It may have been the first memorial tree planted in the Gardens. When that tree died more than a century later, it was replaced by a clone grown from root cuttings taken from the elm: it was planted on 4 May 1979 by Dr John Henry La Trobe, a descendant of Governor La Trobe.

The Separation Tree itself, of course, enjoys the protection of heritage listing and professional maintenance, so its future seems secure. Here's hoping its special status serves to promote the welfare of other grand old trees like it.

The Bicentennial Tree

PEMBERTON, WESTERN AUSTRALIA

Somewhere around the 40-metre mark, my brain urgently suggests a long list of alternatives to what I'm doing right now. It would be a great time, it prompts, to stop climbing this jolly old tree and go get a nice hot cup of tea. Oh, and shouldn't I go back and check if the car's headlights are still on? And, hey, wasn't that the mobile phone ringing in my backpack way down below?

Even if my wretched phone could pick up a signal there's no way I could hear it, up here in this huge tree. The rain is pelting down and the howling wind is playing a castanet symphony on the gum leaves. Anything – anything – would be better than persisting with this cold, wet, miserable, slow and treacherous climb up a bloody great gum tree in the middle of nowhere. I am more than halfway up the so-called ladder on the Dave Evans Bicentennial Tree, a giant karri near Pemberton in Western Australia, designated for unwitting tourists as a 'climbing tree'. Ha! I climbed trees galore as a kid but I never met anything on this scale.

As the name suggests, the tree was adapted for climbing as a Bicentennial project in 1988. It's one of three climbing trees in the region: the other two are the Diamond Tree (51 metres tall) near Manjimup, and the Gloucester Tree (60 metres), Pemberton's most famous tourist attraction. They commemorate the string of tree towers built across the south-west region in the first half of the twentieth century as lookouts for the old enemy – bushfire. In the early 1970s, aircraft took over fire-spotting duties but the towers sometimes are still used for that purpose when aircraft cannot take to the air, or between flights.

The Gloucester Tree attracts around 400,000 climbers a year

They have become extremely popular tourist attractions. Earlier in the day, I had attempted to climb the Gloucester Tree. Official records show that in 1963 some

3000 people climbed this tree, but visitation really took off after 1973 when the original wooden cabin sitting atop the tree was replaced by a steel and aluminium cabin and a visitors' gallery. In 1990, almost 250 000 people visited the tree and about 45 000 of them climbed it. Today, it attracts more than 400 000 people a year, about a quarter of whom climb it for the sheer heck of doing so and for the rewarding views of the surrounding forests. As such, the Gloucester Tree is not only Western Australia's most famous tree but it must be Australia's most-climbed tree as well, with its long-term tally probably running into the millions.

I had gone to the Gloucester Tree first on this rainy day, hoping to add my name to that long list. I had been holed up in a motel for three days, writing while I waited for the sky to clear, but that was all the time I had available. I had to leave first thing next morning. But the rain had just got heavier and the sky was now leaden and the ground awash. To add to my woes, the weather forecast was even grimmer, with strong winds predicted as well. And I had a bit of a tummy bug. But this being my last opportunity to climb the Gloucester Tree, I was going to have to brave it.

The tree is well signposted and just a short drive from Pemberton to the top of a nearby ridge. Ominously, only one other vehicle was in the car park, which on any other day would have been crowded with tourist vehicles. The ranger at the gatehouse gave me a quizzical look when I ducked in from the rain to inquire about climbing conditions. The rain was now bucketing down and the treetops were dancing. 'Actually, there's one group up there now but when they come down I was going to close the tree, because of the conditions,' she said. I was tickled by the idea of a tree that could be closed or opened. I pleaded and explained my mission. She gave me the go-ahead but suggested that if things were too rough here, the Dave Evans Bicentennial Tree might be more sheltered on a day like this. I thanked her and splashed off with a firm resolved to climb at least one of them. 'Take care,' she called after me. 'It's slippery and your hands will get cold if you don't have gloves.' I didn't, of course.

Rain or shine, the Gloucester Tree is a beauty. It was once fifteen metres taller, before it was beheaded to allow the tower to be built atop it. Forester Jack Watson is still remembered for his epic climb to check its suitability. Using climbing boots and a belt slung around its massive seven-metre girth, he took six hours to reach a height of 58 metres, working his way around many limbs, and return. 'This feat is claimed to be a record climb, and is widely recognised in forestry circles as one of the greatest efforts of courage and endurance in the Australian forest,' says the Western Australia Department of Conservation and Land Management fact sheet. Pegging the ladder and lopping the branches was done by another legendary local forester, George Reynolds. Reynolds gradually worked his way up, driving great steel spikes horizontally into the tree in a spiral formation to create the 'ladder'. At one point, a large branch he had cut through twisted and fell onto the ladder below, snapping off a number of pegs and leaving him stranded up the tree. He stayed aloft for several hours while his assistant, Len Nicol, repegged the damaged section from below.

Building watch towers in the treetops required some epic climbs and great courage

As it happened, the then Governor General of Australia, the Duke of Gloucester, was visiting the region at the time. He is said to have greatly enjoyed the spectacle of Reynolds at work while the royal party partook of bush picnic below. Most impressive of all was Reynolds' coolness as he used his axe to lop the top off the tree almost 70 metres above the ground. It's the way of things that the tree and the surrounding national park were named in honour of the toff having the picnic that day, not the bloke who risked life and limb.

As I began to climb that same tree, I came to appreciate Reynold's effort. A flimsy-looking wire mesh was slung on the open side of the ladder, the only thing between me and a nasty fall. I gulped: heights are not my strong point at the best of times but I hadn't expected this. I had imagined an enclosed staircase, with solid steps and sturdy handrails, not a bristled barber's pole. This was no stairway to tree-lover's heaven.

From the base it looks deceptively easy to climb: the sheer size and solidity of these big spikes, deeply embedded into the tree's trunk, confer confidence and they give only a little under your weight. It's like a steepish spiral staircase, with no treads and no handrails. But by the time I'd reached the twenty-metre mark I was none too happy: I was drenched, my shoes were slipping on the spikes and I was finding it hard to grip because my hands were getting stiff with the cold.

At that point, the descending feet of the two German tourists who had been up the tree hove into view around the trunk. They were white-knuckled, teeth chattering and most politely insistent that it was not particularly safe for me to proceed. Nein. I had to agree. The wind was gusting more strongly now and leaves and twigs were beginning to rain down as well.

So that was how I'd come to this even bigger beast of a karri, the David Evans Bicentennial Tree, and why I wasn't going to listen to my feeble, cowardly brain. I had earlier reached the 25-metre mark in style, standing with pathetic gratitude on the rest-platform there. Through the torrent of rain I thought I could make out the forest understorey, a jungle-like tangle of vines . . . or something like that.

Now I am more than halfway up and

No handrails or steps, just a spiral of steel spikes

I press on, cursing the worsening weather. As you monkey up – both hands and feet are required – the big solid mass of wood to your left is more than reassuring. This is, after all, a species known for its very hard wood. This particular tree is a cracker in the prime of its life, a mere 220 years old, or thereabouts. This one has followed the 'karri recipe' to the letter. It has grown straight, strong and true, a model of rectitude and stability. Except in high winds: I now found it extraordinary that such a large tree could lean and sway so much.

I am now having difficulty on several fronts. My hands are very stiff and, although I can cope with the flurries of wet leaves dropping on me, the long sodden ribbons of bark splatting around me are more disconcerting. I swear loudly whenever this happens, with no possibility of offending anyone. Anyone except the Bicentennial Tree, that is: I seem to have hurt its feelings because now it summons up even gustier winds and is shaking its head in anger.

I get the unnerving feeling that it wants to toss me off and is bucking like a rodeo bull. But I persist, rung by bloody rung, and call out defiantly: 'You won't get rid of me that easily!' I immediately regret my taunt because, having failed to dislodge me by swaying, it now starts raining down larger missiles. Sticks and strips of bark tumble past as I press closer into its flank, sliding my shoulder up it as I complete another circuit of this wretched barber's pole.

Just as my confidence is returning, a huge strip of sodden bark plummets down and slaps me hard and loud on the head. The shock almost causes me to lose my grip. Now you've got my attention, Dave, I can tell you: even if the chicken wire can stop me from tumbling sideways – and I have no confidence that it can – the thought of falling onto the spikes below and breaking an arm or a leg is not good. It's unlikely I can count on help arriving for some time and if I were to whack my head in the process, well . . . Taking stock, I squint up into the rain to see how much further I must go to reach the top viewing platform. I can do this, I think, I'm just spooked by a bit of bark. This time I say nothing to Dave, but he is onto me and this time he isn't kidding around. It isn't a particularly big branch, to be sure, but it is straight and solid, with a jagged tip where it had snapped off above me. It spears past me so close that if it hadn't been blowing a gale, I would have heard it whistle.

So, I am sorry, dear reader, but that did it: I yielded to commonsense and descended as quickly and carefully as I could. The wind was growing stronger and more and more debris was coming down. I stood shivering in the nearby shelter and wondered whether I had got Dave all wrong: perhaps he wasn't being a cranky old karri at all but trying to save me from myself. Who knows? Maybe this is all just fanciful stuff from the feverish mind of a chicken-livered, rain-drenched traveller far from home.

Trees with vision

The Cazneaux Tree

WILPENA POUND, SOUTH AUSTRALIA

One day when the sun shone hot and strong, I stood before this giant in silent wonder and admiration. The hot wind stirred the leafy boughs and some of the living elements of this tree passed to me in understanding and friendliness expressing the spirit of Australia.

Harold Cazneaux (1878–1953)

Out of the frying-pan flatness and sultry heat of the plains country 400 kilometres north of Adelaide, the remarkable Wilpena Pound rises proudly in a craggy spectacle of purple ridges and overhanging bluffs. This crater-shaped geological wonder is the worn-down stump of what was once a Himalayan-sized dome of mountain. Its remnants form a giant natural amphitheatre that has been likened to a lost world. The ever-changing colours of these hard and ancient rocks are often splashed with glowing groves of golden wattle and vivid dots of red, purple and pink from desert pea and desert rose, hopbush and bottlebrush.

Of the many thousands of gum trees in and around Wilpena, one has gained a place all its own in Australian history. It has no glamorous flowers or unusual traits. It's not a rare species, nor especially tall. It's not particularly ancient or distinctive. Truth be told, this tree has achieved greatness just by being there. Or at least, by being there at a special moment when a great photographer's mind was open to the possibility of seeing greatness. Captured in that moment, this tree came to symbolise something profound, inspiring and hope-filled for millions of people around the world.

The photographer's name was Harold Cazneaux. He died more than 50 years ago – on 19 June 1953 – but the tree that bears his name lives on. That is only fitting, since

Facing page: Spirit of Endurance: Cazneaux captured its bare-knuckle grip on life

Seventy years later, the Cazneaux Tree is still hanging on

he called the hardy old river red gum in the unforgettable photograph he took in 1937 'Spirit of Endurance'.

The Cazneaux tree itself is today even more battered and scarred by the elements than it was back then, with its gaping hollow trunk, gnarled limbs and bare-knuckle grip on the soil. Most of its crown is gone and a recent drought seems to have hastened the balding process. But subsequent rain has seen it sprout a thick new crop of leaves from its base – testimony to the amazing resilience of life. No wonder young lovers occasionally get married beneath its boughs.

Cazneaux's photographic legacy lives on as well, although – strangely – no major exhibition was arranged for the 50th anniversary of the death of a man Max Dupain once called 'the father of modern Australian photography'.

Cazneaux was born to Australian parents – both photographers – in New Zealand in 1878. The family moved to Adelaide about 1889 and young Harold later found studio work as a photographic colourist and retoucher. But he preferred the creative freedom of art to the contrived formality of studio photography. He liked sketching and drawing and took evening classes at the Adelaide School of Art and Design in the hope of a making a career that way.

But when he was twenty his ambition changed: an international exhibition of photographs featuring the work of the new Pictorial Movement inspired him to revisit photography. The Pictorialists thought of a camera as an aesthetic tool, much like a paintbrush, to be used to create a work of art. Admiring their soft impressionistic focus, Cazneaux apparently realised for the first time that he could express his own artistic sentiments through the lens of a camera.

He left Adelaide in 1904 to work in a Sydney photographic studio and began a double life. Six days a week he was a studio journeyman, but in whatever time he could squeeze out of what was left over – travelling to and from work, during meal breaks and on Sundays – he experimented vigorously as a photographic artist recording the lives, times and places he encountered.

It soon became apparent that he had a unique eye for seeing the extraordinary in the ordinary – workers sardined neatly into their ferry seats, burly wharfies on the docks or rock fishermen pitting themselves against the sea. At first he had to process film in his own laundry; not having electricity, he used daylight to expose his prints. But his talent and creativity with photographic processes quickly won him better access to darkrooms.

By 1909 his output had been so impressive that he was invited to stage Australia's first one-man photographic exhibition in the rooms of the Photographic Society of New South Wales, establishing him as a rising force in the field. It wasn't long before he was winning competitions, opening his own studio, and photographing the people, homes and gardens of the rich and famous for Home magazine, as well as everyday city life, native plants and animals.

Cazneaux helped to found a small but influential group of photographers who called themselves the Sydney Camera Circle: they 'pledged to work and to advance pictorial photography and to show our own Australia in terms of sunlight rather than those of greyness and dismal shadows'. He catalogued the building of the Sydney Harbour Bridge from beginning to end. Then a commission from the BHP company took him back to South Australia in 1935, to document the building of the Whyalla steelworks. The mountain ranges he saw in the distance called out to him and he experienced a new, perhaps even mystical, feeling.

'They sent me in my Buick car up to Iron Knob near Port Augusta, S.A.,' he later recalled. 'There I saw and felt the impulse of the great inland Central Australia. The mysterious Flinders Range dominated the skyline.' In that same year, the artist Hans Heysen held an exhibition in Sydney. Heysen had made many trips into the Flinders Ranges in previous years, refining his discerning eye for gum trees in particular. His evocative and quintessentially Australian paintings filled Cazneaux with admiration. One in particular, *Red Gums of the Far North* – which won the Wynne Prize – inspired him to try to capture with his camera something of that same vision.

He wrote to Heysen seeking counsel for a proposed trip to the ranges: 'No one handles foliage like yourself of our gums as seen against the sky or against the light,' he wrote. 'You do this with such great simplicity. I feel that I already know your far north country from your pictures, and armed with your personal advice to me I intend to go there at my first opportunity in the near future.' The two men went on to become friends.

Cazneaux's commercial success had made it possible for him to take time to travel inland more often in search of rural scenes to put on film, but floods and dust-storms frustrated his first attempt to answer the siren call of those distant ranges. But in 1937 he was back there – with his wife Winifred and teenage son Harold – wide-eyed at the ever-changing light, the extraordinary organic forms and the majesty of the trees. Pausing on a hill midway along the ranges near Wilpena Pound, he spied a gum below – a river red gum that stood alone on the banks of a watercourse – that somehow demanded his attention. He decided to take a closer look.

A few years later he recorded his first close and romantic encounter with that tree. It was a life-changing moment in which he felt something spiritual from the land itself enter his soul. Here's how he described it:

> This giant gum tree stands in solitary grandeur on a lonely plateau in the arid Flinders Ranges, South Australia, where it has grown up from a sapling through the years, and long before the shade from its giant limbs ever gave shelter from the heat to white men. The passing of the years has left it scarred and marked by the elements – storm, fire, water – unconquered, it speaks to us from a Spirit of Endurance. Although aged, its widespread limbs speak of a vitality that will carry on for many more years. One day, when the sun shone hot and strong, I stood before this giant in silent wonder and admiration. The hot wind stirred the leafy boughs and some of the living elements of this tree passed to me in understanding and friendliness expressing the Spirit of Australia.

In that instant of bonding, Cazneaux pointed his camera, clicked the shutter and somehow captured the powerful emotion he felt. He did not stand well back to fit the tree's shaggy crown into the frame, but concentrated instead on its hollowed-out trunk and broad base. It was a device probably inspired by Heysen, who often framed gums so that their canopies were incomplete, to let the viewer's gaze rise off the top of the page and imagine the union of leaf and light, earth and sky.

The clincher here for Cazneaux was the tree's remarkable root system. It had been exposed from the soil on one side by the undercutting action of an ephemeral creek. The roots resembled nothing so much as wizened old hands – fingers clutching white-knuckled onto the creek bank for their life. To let go meant death, to hold on with steely determination was the very nub of survival.

This was no mere photograph – it was art of great insight, a frank, intuitive and direct personal portrait. Cazneaux's eye had found a way somehow to represent an essence of a quality that was not only uniquely Australian but also universal in its appeal. His success was immediately recognised by critics, colleagues and ordinary people alike, and the photograph's timeless truth and power resonated far beyond Australia's shores. In 1938 he was made an honorary fellow of the Royal Photographic

Society of Great Britain. The Spirit of Endurance was exhibited many times in Australia and elsewhere. It went on to become one of the world's most popular calendar and postcard photographs of any tree.

In a sad twist of fate, his son Harold had a copy of the picture with him when he was killed in fighting at Tobruk during World War II. Cazneaux never quite recovered from the loss. Even so, he did not lose interest in his tree. He later wrote to a resident of Wilpena to ask if 'that grand old tree still stood there'. It did indeed, came the reply, and it was now known as the Cazneaux Tree and would be cared for. He told Heysen: 'Well, if I ever had a lift up this news gave it to me.'

The catalogue notes for a touring exhibition of Cazneaux's work in the mid-1990s, assembled by the National Library of Australia – which holds the main archive of Cazneaux prints and negatives – and the Historic Houses Trust of New South Wales, described his highly individual photographs as 'timeless in their creative beauty and their extraordinary tonal qualities'.

Today, the Cazneaux Tree is a much-loved and much-visited Flinders icon – a compulsory photo stop for countless tourists. It personifies river red gums as 'ancient, stained and warty' trees that are 'barnacled with legends', as author Murray Bail has said of them. The nation's most widespread eucalypt has been witness to so much of our history. To sit with the Cazneaux Tree in the deep quiet of sunset watching the ever-changing hues of blue, purple and gold play across the walls of Wilpena Pound is to share in that briefest of moments when a great tree and a great mind met.

Trees with vision

Namatjira's trees

CENTRAL AUSTRALIA, NORTHERN TERRITORY

When I approached, he was seated with his companions around a fire. It was just an ordinary native camp, such as I have seen many hundreds of times – a low windbreak of boughs, a line of smouldering fires with hollows between them where the men had slept the night before, spears and shields leaning against the bushes, and pieces of cooked euro meat in the forks of the trees nearby . . . from under that windbreak Albert took a parcel of beautiful watercolours, wrapped in a clean cloth to show me. He leaned them against a low bush, one by one (for he was too good an artist to show them together), and then stood to one side so that his shadow would relieve the glare of the bright inland sunlight.

Charles P. Mountford, anthropologist

Albert Namatjira blazed many new trails. In 1939, one of his watercolours, *Illum-baura (Haasts Bluff), Central Australia* became the first work of art by an Aborigine to be acquired by an Australian gallery, rather than by a museum. He was the first Aborigine to be listed in *Who's Who in Australia*. In 1953, he was awarded the Queen's Coronation Medal and was the first Aborigine to be presented to the Queen, at a ceremony at Government House the following year. In 1957, Albert and his wife Rubina were the first indigenous Australians to be granted full citizenship, after a public outcry over his being denied the right to buy a house, solely because he was an Aborigine. Two years later he died despairing and dispirited after being jailed on charges (which he denied and had appealed all the way to the High Court) of supplying alcohol to a fellow Aborigine. His early death, aged 57, robbed the world of an exceptional man with a unique gift.

Namatjira was to be the first artist to find a way to show urban Australians the richness and complexity that lay at the supposed 'dead heart' of their continent. The warmth, depth and subtlety of his watercolours portrayed an almost magical world that most city-dwelling Australians had never seen or imagined. Once they saw his evocative paintings of wonderful places in the Northern Territory – such as Glen Helen Gorge, Mount Sonder, Haasts Bluff, Heavitree Gap, Standley Chasm and Palm Valley – they wanted to see his country for themselves. It's hard to believe today that these grand, ancient and beautiful landscapes – now tourist magnets – were barely known at all outside the world of Namatjira's youth. His great talent was his ability to set down on paper a way of seeing his country in all its nuances of colour, light, shape and splendour.

I have visited many of the places Namatjira painted. Watching transfixed as the sun set over the MacDonnell Ranges – with its long, slow, beautiful play of light and shade, the delicate wax and wane of shifting hues of mauve, pink, green and orange – was so moving it made my heart thump and brought tears to my eyes. The photographs I brought home could not do it justice. Yet through Namatjira's work I am somehow transported back there, to that rarefied light, the high vault of the sky and great faraway sense of distance and space. They are not just paintings; they have an extra quality that is very special: you are not merely looking at a scene as an outside observer, you are being drawn into it as a participant. All this with a few deft dabs of coloured water.

What set Namatjira apart from other Aboriginal artists at the time was his unique adoption of white-man's art materials and styles. That alone made his art approachable for non-Aborigines. The grandeur of the landscapes he depicted also had its own allure. But the reason Namatjira finds a place in this book is for his special way of looking at the trees of the arid zone. Scan through a collection of his work and you'll see them everywhere: acacias dotted across a rolling line of hills, snaking green trails along a dried-up watercourse, a desert bloodwood festooned with creamy flowers, aged mulgas snug between boulders or a stand of perky native cypress pines. Indeed, it's a rare Namatjira that doesn't feature some kind of tree somewhere.

Among his most famous works are those in which a tree is the central feature. The rare and remarkable Livistona palms of Palm Valley, for example, were among his most popular subjects. Their eye-pleasing geometric mop-top foliage, set against a clear blue sky and propped on long, thin wonky stems, is captured so simply that it belies the effort he took to capture them in a certain way. He would camp there for days, going back to the same spot at the same time of day to observe a trick of light and a particular angle of the sun. He had a special personal connection with Palm Valley

– now part of Finke Gorge National Park – since he had kutungula, or 'manager', status for that country by inheritance through his mother, Ljukutja.

Namatjira's parents were Arrernte people who left a traditional life to live at the Hermannsburg Lutheran Mission, near Alice Springs. He was born there in 1902 and named Elea, but was christened Albert when his parents became Christians. When he was thirteen he was taken from the mission for six months to be initiated into Arrernte community and taught traditional law and custom. For the rest of his life he seemed at ease with maintaining dual Christian and traditional beliefs, even though that could puzzle and disquiet others. Anthropologist Charles Mountford later portrayed Namatjira as one of the few people who could span both the black and white worlds. On one occasion when the artist had just completed one of his watercolours, he began telling Mountford about his Dreaming place and of secret men's business that happened there. The scientist was surprised that Namatjira knew the symbolic art and imagery that went with it and was even more surprised when he offered to draw it. 'It was surely an experience without parallel to watch a man depicting, in the most primitive of all arts, beliefs that stretched back to the dawn of creation, while lying beside him, the product of the same hand, were beautiful watercolours in the art of today.' Perhaps one of Namatjira's legacies is that the capacity to hold two complementary world views is no longer seen as freakish.

In any case, the trees that Namatjira seemed to paint with most feeling and character were those of his own country. He inherited from his father's side the oasis waterholes of Ormiston Gorge, the captivating mauves of the 'sleeping lady' – Mount Sonder – and the fiery red rocks of Glen Helen. Here he painted what were essentially intimate portraits – not of people but of individual trees. They were exceptional studies in personality. His 1954 *Glowing Monarch* shows a mighty river red gum with wrinkled bark like an old man's skin, and an old man's paunch as well. It's literally a warts-and-all image, with a radiant light on one side of its pale trunk in early or late daylight. Cruddy bits of dead bark adhere to its base or cling within its furrows, and it bristles with knobby lumps where old limbs have been shed and healed over. Barely any leaves are shown; the canopy is so heavily cropped that just a few dabs of the brush reveal them dangling down at the top of the frame of view, as if to confirm that this veteran eucalypt is indeed alive. The image is all about the trunk and the cryptic story it has to tell of survival. Like the one in Cazneaux's *Spirit of Endurance*, this is an otherwise unexceptional tree made special by being so well observed.

But the main reason I rank Namatjira's trees among Australia's greatest is his feel for the character of the stunning ghost gums. They are a favourite of photographers for the contrast between the bleached whiteness of their trunks and the reds of the

soil and stone. At times they seem to writhe up out of the bare rocks in the most improbable of places, perched perilously on the edge of clifftop or defying gravity midway up a sheer rock wall. Namatjira painted some of these more obvious subjects, but sometimes his choices were surprising. One he painted towards the end of his life, for example – *Ghost gum Mt Sonder, MacDonnell Ranges* – is a mere slip of thing with a trunk so wayward and wonky it looks like it's been run over by a truck, then twisted and wrung out by giant's hands. Spindly dead branches fan out across the top of the frame and other skeletal dead trees dot the foreground but they cleverly lead your eye to the faraway mountain. It is bathed in a wash of purplish lavender but finely detailed just the same: you can count half a dozen different hues of the same colour where Namatjira deftly picks out its ridges and spurs as they throw shadow or catch the light. Gaze into the scene and you feel as though you are there, pausing in the sparse shade of this gangly tree on your journey towards the great sleeping lady. As another great Australian artist, Lloyd Rees, once phrased it: 'I respond deeply to the Namatjira vision. I find in his work a marvellous sense of distance and space. His eye can look so far away and seem to know what's there.'

Most often, though, Namatjira would choose a big old ghost gum as his foreground subject, usually – but not always – placed a little to the left or right. It was a device he learned from Rex Batterbee, the artist who first exposed Namatjira to watercolour painting in 1934 by holding an exhibition at Hermannsburg Mission. So intrigued was the young man that he acquired his own paints and paper. In May 1935 he presented a painting as a gift to a member of the Lutheran Mission Board. Years later, when shown it again, he wrote on it: 'This is my first painting.' In 1936, Batterbee came back and hired Namatjira as his guide and camel handler. In return, the artist gave him two months of art lessons, which he mastered with great speed and skill. 'Albert quickly understood the rules of perspective, composition, and the way of seeing colour and setting it down on paper,' Batterbee wrote. 'He understood and utilised the fundamentals of art that had taken some people many years to learn.'

Batterbee became one of his chief promoters and within a few years Namatjira's work was being exhibited and snapped up in the major cities. Namatjira's trees are a lasting bequest of his vision, and his ghost gums lie at the core of that bequest. He captures the individual in each of them. Red-brown stains run down their flanks where some insect has bored in and been repelled by the tree's keno defences. Where stout limbs part company with the trunk, his brush picks out those soft flesh-like folds. Furrows, grooves, hollows, amputated branches with blackened stumps and an abrupt collar of gorgeous white bark – these are traits and quirks that any Australian would feel familiar with in gum trees across the country. Ghost gums had other significance to Aboriginal people. The keno was softened in water and used as a glue for assembling weapons and tools or to repair cracked implements. The fine powdery substance that gives the bark its unique whiteness was used to decorate and colour ornaments and body art. Western Arrernte people had a special use for a naturally hollow branch – not as a didgeridoo but as an amplifier for a song of love sorcery. Namatjira's magic is there for all to see in the spell cast by this great Australian tree.

Old, older . . . .
oldest?

The Meelup Mallee

BUSSELTON, WESTERN AUSTRALIA

When botanist Neville Marchant discovered the Meelup Mallee in 1981, it would be an understatement to say that the future did not look promising for this dwarf eucalypt. For starters, its ranks were very thin: a mere 27 plants were clustered in a small area of scrub on a sandy ridge overlooking the sea west of Busselton, in south-western Australia. Each plant consisted of a clump of stems about five metres high, a typical mallee formation. There had been more trees growing there but now a gravel road led straight to the site and a scenic lookout and car park had been built smack dab in the middle of them.

It was understandable that no one had noticed anything special about them. Clumps of mallees with multiple stems, blue-green leaves and creamy flowers are unremarkable in this part of the world. The fact that this one had slightly unusual corky bark was not enough to single it out for attention to other than expert eyes. Worse still was the condition of these trees: they were suffering from a fungal infection, they were riddled with cankers that split open their stems and they were under threat from termite and borer attacks. Worst of all was the realisation that their ranks were even thinner than first thought.

DNA fingerprinting revealed that all 27 plants were genetically identical – they were clones. The apparently distinct trees visible on the surface were just ramets, or separate pieces of the same plant, sprouting from a slowly spreading root system. Despite extensive searches since, not another Meelup Mallee has been found, so the entire species consists of just this one individual. They don't come any rarer than that.

The next shock came when researchers worked out the plant's age. It couldn't be done by counting growth rings on one of the stems, because that stem would be far younger than the plant itself: mallees sprout vigorously after a fire, for example, sending up new stems from a large woody underground root (a lignotuber). So the best way to age it was to work out the dimensions of the mallee root and the annual rate at which it was likely to have spread: divide the former by the latter and you have its approximate age in years. While this method is nowhere near as precise as counting growth rings, it is an accepted and reasonably scientific way of estimating the age of mallees that have this fairy-ring pattern of spreading. Since this plant extended over almost a hectare, it was already clear that it was quite old. When the numbers came in, however, jaws dropped. One scientist estimated that it was 6380 years old, while a second put it at 6660 years old: the average was 6520.

In short, tourists visiting the lookout to gaze down on the sea were unwittingly standing in, perhaps even on, one of the rarest and oldest living things on the planet.

Things look much brighter for the Meelup Mallee today, but boosting its survival chances has been a complex and sustained process. In the ensuing 25 years it has won legal protection as a critically endangered species. A formal recovery plan is being implemented. The lookout has been closed and its carpark ripped up. Special 'declared rare flora' markers have been placed at the site to deter accidental damage. Dashboard stickers and posters have been produced to alert members of the public. Volunteers and public officials routinely monitor the site. A special fire response strategy has even been incorporated into the region's overall fire control plan: while some fires may stimulate its growth, a severe fire could be catastrophic.

The mallee's stems have been treated for their borers, cankers and fungal infections, although some still split and die. Tissue samples have been taken: some have been stored in deep freeze and others have been propagated successfully using tissue-culture technology, the artificial version of the plant's own natural cloning method. Best of all, in 2003 scientists were able to collect seed from the plant for the first time since its discovery. They were able to germinate three of them and get them growing. They may, of course, be hybrids resulting from cross-pollination with another species. The Meelup Mallee – *Eucalyptus phylacis* – may itself by a hybrid, since it appears to be closely related to another mallee, *Eucalyptus decipiens*. If there was another parent species it has not been found despite extensive searches in the region, meaning that it might be extinct. At least its offspring, the unique Meelup Mallee, now seems to have avoided that fate.

Old, older . . . oldest?

The Mongarlowe Mallee

SOUTHERN TABLELANDS, NEW SOUTH WALES

For a pint-sized little runt of a tree – often no taller than an adult man, but a tree nevertheless – the Mongarlowe Mallee has a giant claim to fame. It first came to light in 1985, thanks to a sharp-eyed local landholder who noticed it growing in the bush near Mongarlowe, in the Southern Tablelands of New South Wales. Like many mallees, the *Eucalyptus recurra* consisted of multiple stems from a common woody root bole (mallee root is legendary as hard, long-burning firewood). When its scientific description was published in 1988, the Mongarlowe Mallee was said to be the 'rarest of all' eucalypts. What grabbed international headlines, though, was the suggestion that this individual might be of an immense age, predating the dawn of human agriculture and perhaps the oldest known living thing on the planet. Someone dubbed it the Ice Age Gum, and the tree's place in the world's record books has been discussed and debated in many forums. It has even been cited as a key piece of evidence with which to refute Noah's Flood and biblical Creationism.

Since the first find, three more sites have come to light. A second plant in the Mongarlowe area was discovered in 1990 by a consultant doing a flora survey for the proposed Welcome Reef Dam. Four years later, a consultant doing a similar survey for a clay-mining development found another plant at nearby Windellama, 30 kilometres away, and a second smaller plant not previously noticed there was found in 2001. Also in 2001 another tree was found near Mongarlowe during a special helicopter survey conducted by the National Parks and Wildlife Service. No more have been found since, despite plenty of searching, so the sum total of the species is just five plants. Its status as the rarest eucalypt has been lost, since we now know the Meelup Mallee consists of just one genetic individual.

The trees grow in stunted heath country amid casuarina, hakea, tea-tree and banksias, taking what nourishment they can from shallow sandy soils overlying heavy clay. They flower erratically – some prolifically and others barely at all – and only sometimes produce a small number of seeds, which is not unusual among mallees. Not a single seedling has been found in the wild. They seem to hybridise readily with other eucalypt species, probably as a result of insect cross-pollination. That means that even when they do produce viable seed the results are discouraging for scientists trying to propagate the species to better secure its existence.

In 1992, for example, CSIRO researchers successfully raised 47 seedlings from seed collected from the two plants known at that time. Only thirteen of them physically resembled their Mongarlowe Mallee parents and only eight of those survived until they were ready to be planted out the following year, at a research arboretum near Canberra; all of them died within a year. The remaining 34 seedlings flourished and, by 1999, many were four metres tall and had begun producing flower buds; unfortunately, the shape of the flowers disclosed that these were hybrids with a parent from another species, most likely a black swamp gum.

Because the individual Mongarlowe Mallee stands are no closer than two kilometres to each other, they have little chance of a successful long-distance affair: it's asking a lot of a moth, fly or beetle to carry pollen from one Mongarlowe Mallee to another. When they were hand-pollinated from an unrelated Mongarlowe Mallee, however, some healthy and 'pure' offspring were produced.

The scientist most closely acquainted with the Mongarlowe Mallee is John Briggs, an expert in threatened species. When I asked him about the claims of great age for this tree he was suitably cautious. Its age is uncertain, although it is certainly very old, he says. It is at least hundreds of years and may well be thousands of years old. The official draft recovery plan for the species explains why the uncertainty exists. It points out that the five plants vary considerably in size. The smallest has only twenty stems, none taller than an average adult man. The largest, at Windemalla, has almost 80 stems, ranging in height from 1.5 to 2.8 metres. They emerge from a massive mallee root twelve metres long and five metres wide. Just as the bulk of an iceberg is unseen beneath the waves, most of the action in a mallee is below ground: this one is a real doozey.

It is the great size and bulk of this root that confirms the great age of the plant. As it expands, a mallee root develops new buds on its leading edge and from these the plant can send up new stems as needed. In this case, the local conditions and lack of soil nutrients mean that the root is unlikely to grow by more than two millimetres a year, meaning that it would have taken some 3000 years to attain its present spread. As the

old, older . . . oldest?

plan explains: 'There is also a possibility that the two plants near Windellama, located 40 metres apart, are identical genotypes that originated from a common rootstock that separated and spread in different directions. If this were demonstrated to be the case then the above calculation applied to a minimum migration distance of 26 metres would give this plant an age of 13 000 years.' Wow! They don't come much older than that.

So the oldest Mongarlowe Mallee may be a real Methuselah, a tree that did indeed start its life right back in the depths of the last Ice Age. If other satellite pieces of the Windemalla mallee root – alive or dead – were to be found even further away from the main section, it could be older still. But that's speculation: based on what we already know, the Mongarlowe Mallee certainly deserves a proud place among Australia's greatest trees. Even at the minimum age of 3000 years it outstrips most other trees anywhere in the world. Australia's native conifers are often cited for their longevity but even Huon pines rarely exceed 2000 years, while King Billy pines can live for 1200 years and celery-top pines for about 800 years.

According to an erroneous fact sheet on the website of the Parks and Wildlife Service, Tasmania, Huon pine is 'Australia's oldest living tree' and 'only the bristle-cone pine of North America exceeds it in age.' It asserts that some individual Huon pines have been known to reach an age of 3000 years, while a fossilised specimen found in a boggy area of the state's south-west was 'dated at 3462 years!' That's mighty impressive but the Meelup Mallee alone is almost twice as old and the Mongarlowe Mallee may be almost four times older than the oldest Huon pine.

I hasten to add here that a large and remarkable stand of 300 Huon pines growing on the flanks of Mount Read in Tasmania has been widely reported as being over 10 000 years old. This may be true – personally, I'd love to believe it is – but that claim also rests largely on the fact that all the individuals in the stand are genetically identical males (the species has male and female plants) that arose from one or more individuals that have continued to grow by vegetative reproduction. Sediments in a nearby lake are said to reveal a continuous record going back 10 500 years of pollen from these same trees. There's no doubt that Huon pines can spread by cloning themselves. A low branch that touches the ground can take root and eventually establish itself as a new tree. Even a fallen branch can do so under the right circumstances. In an environment like Mount Read, high winds and the weight of winter snow can generate many broken branches. None of the stems in the stand is older than about 1,500 years, so doubt remains about how long it has taken for the stand as a whole to develop. At the very least though, the Mount Read trees are old by any standard and collectively they are a spectacular example of a clone the size of a city block. The mountain itself is a veritable museum of Australian conifers – eight of Tasmania's nine species grow there – and is a window back into our ancient Gondwanan heritage.

As for the Mongarlowe Mallee, its future seems unclear. Each of the stands grows on private land and most have been at potential risk in recent times from projects as diverse as dam-building, mineral extraction and a commercial rubbish dump. But the species now at least enjoys the formal protection of listing as endangered under New South Wales and Federal law, and the landholders have a track record of being co-operative to conservation efforts on behalf of the tree. As well, the work put into understanding its biology and its propagation means that a single calamity is now unlikely to wipe it from the face of the earth. Botanic gardens across the world will doubtless be glad to grow more as suitable material becomes available. In any case, the five trees have surely proved their hardiness, since they must have experienced and survived scores of bushfires during their long lives.

Yet a real question mark hangs over their long-term future in the wild. Because all five stands occur in largely uncleared and unaltered country not suited to agriculture, these trees are rare not as a result of human activity, but are naturally so. Why? Most likely, they are the last of a species that was once more extensive but has been in decline for a long time. They may have evolved under very different climatic conditions, for example, and were unable to adapt as things changed. Perhaps those that remain are an exceptionally hardy few with especially persistent lignotubers that enable them to keep sprouting new stems even though their physical separation means they can no longer reproduce sexually with their own kind. Meanwhile, they are at least still capable of interbreeding with other gums and so may pass on some of their DNA into the great eucalypt gene pool. But one day, presumably, these five little trees with their massive wooden keels will reach the end of their individual journeys and sprout no more. Mind you, there's no telling how far distant that day may be: another 13 000 years?

Old, older . . . oldest?

The Wollemi Pine

WOLLEMI NATIONAL PARK, NEW SOUTH WALES

I was daydreaming, staring from the window on the 27th floor of the building where I worked at the *Sydney Morning Herald*. The spectacular view stretched west across the city all the way to the Great Dividing Range, strung out across the horizon like a line of blue caterpillars. Whenever I saw it, my thoughts went back to teenage adventures in those mountains, hiking along the rugged Grose River valley: close encounters with huge goannas, skinny-dipping in the clear cold water, wind roaring through the massive gum trees … A familiar voice jerked me back to reality. I turned to see our Environment Reporter, James Woodford, red-faced, grinning and waving his notebook at me: 'I've got it, and it's a great story!' he said, barely able to contain his excitement. It was indeed a great story, and it concerned a tree in those same Blue Mountains.

It was mid-December 1994, and I was the *Herald*'s Science and Environment Editor. As Woodford detailed the remarkable discovery of the Wollemi pine, I was on the edge of my chair. A few months earlier, he explained, three adventurous bushwalkers – David Noble, Michael Casteleyn and Tony Zimmerman – had hiked and abseiled their way into one of the most remote parts of the Wollemi wilderness. Even though it is little more than 100 kilometres from Sydney, it is a landscape so rugged and forbidding that many of its vast maze of gorges, ridges and canyons have been disturbed rarely, if ever, by people. It's about as close as you can come these days to a lost world, an undisturbed part of old Australia, and so close to the nation's largest city.

All three hikers were experienced, but Noble knew these mountains as well as anyone and was a natural leader. He led the group into a canyon he had visited recently but this time from its opposite end. It was tough going. At times they needed ropes

Old, older … oldest?

to descend sheer rockfaces. In other places they needed to strip off to plunge across creeks fed by icy springs welling up from deep underground. At one point, as they approached a shady rainforest gully with sheer rock on either side, Noble came to a halt. There was something odd, something different about it.

As he later recounted, Noble saw ahead of him a group of large trees. Amid the usual coachwood, sassafras, lilly pilly and ferns, his eye was drawn to some unfamiliar trees with broad cylindrical trunks covered with a weird bark: it was brown and had a bubbled surface texture that reminded him of Coco Pops, the children's chocolate-flavoured rice cereal. The leaves were unusual as well, with a deep green fern-like appearance, and they created a heaped leaf litter that he had not seen before. The hikers took in the scene then, as they prepared to push on, Noble intuitively snapped off a small piece of a young green branch to take with him. His parents had given him a keen interest in botany. But John Noble, who had an extensive knowledge of plants, didn't recognise the now dry and crushed cutting his son showed him two days later. Next it was shown to Wyn Jones, a senior naturalist with the New South Wales National Parks and Wildlife Service, where David Noble also worked. Jones thought it might be a fern until Noble told him: 'It's from a bloody big tree.'

Jones eliminated one possibility after another and consulted colleagues, who were equally in the dark or could only speculate as to its identity. So Jones went to the canyon with Noble to see for himself, arriving late in the afternoon on 15 October. He was astonished. Tall slim pines soared above him, more than twenty handsome trees of a kind he had never seen the like of. Some were well over 30 metres tall and had trunks a metre across. Their foliage was arranged in spiralling twists along their branches, and there were strange knobs on the ends of the highest branches as well and flat-leafed seedlings growing among large fallen trunks on the gully floor. With cameras and notebooks, the party eagerly recorded what they could before dark fell, taking more leaf and bark samples with them when they left.

After more than 200 years of European settlement, here was a tree that no one had seen before, a species new to science and a major discovery in its own right. But as it turned out it was far more significant than that. Within weeks, researchers from the Royal Botanic Gardens, Sydney, were as excited as Jones. It wasn't just that this was an entirely new species of conifer, but that the nearest known tree to it was a fossil – they had one right there in Sydney, in the Australian Museum – and was thought to have become extinct millions of years earlier. Here was the plant world's equivalent of a living, breathing dinosaur that had come back to life. Noble had stumbled across one of the botanical finds of the century, up there with the discovery of two other living fossils, the gingko and the dawn redwood.

The first Wollemi pine saplings awaiting auction at Sydney's Royal Botanic Gardens in 2005

It was a like a movie script and Woodford had it on his own, with pictures. Part of my job as his boss was to 'sell' his story to the Herald's afternoon news conference, to persuade them of its significance and make sure it got a prominent run. It was the easiest sale I ever made. Woodford wrote the draft and we worked on it together, trying hard not to let enthusiasm get in the way of allowing this remarkable story to speak for itself. For the full ripping yarn, I urge you to read James Woodford's book *The Wollemi Pine: the Incredible Discovery of a Living Fossil from the Age of the Dinosaurs*.

Stories like that don't come along every day in the news business, nor do they in the science business. There was something about it that tweaked everyone's excitement, and trees don't often do that, not in the heart-touching way that animals do. Perhaps the nature of its discovery rang a communal bell – the bold young adventurer going off into the wilderness and returning with colourful tales of strange encounters is a familiar plot in folk stories the world over. Perhaps it was the captivating thought that in a world increasingly crowded with people and hooked on technology, great natural wonders and mysteries are still 'out there' for those who care to look. Perhaps it was because the tree is so big and humans are strangely obsessed with big things: whales, elephants and polar bears get far more attention than they deserve. Then there was the fact that this is a conifer, one of humanity's favourite groups of trees, and an aesthetically appealing one at that.

Whatever it was, the Wollemi pine was instantly a massive story across the world. News reporters besieged the key players, bushwalkers tried to find its secret location, wild rumours flew of a private collector willing to pay $500 000 for a so-called 'Pinosaur' and of plans for secret raids by foreign plant-nappers. Everyone wanted to see one, touch one or own one. It emerged as well that scientists had come tantalisingly close to discovering it earlier while searching for new plants in Wollemi National Park: Wyn Jones himself and John Benson from the Royal Botanic Gardens had missed the canyon by a few hundred metres on separate occasions a decade or so earlier. The romance and the intrigue just grew and grew around this amazing tree, now officially named after the place and the person associated with its discovery, *Wollemia nobilis*.

Much has now been learnt about the Wollemi pine. Best of all, a second population of the pines has been found in another canyon not far away, bringing the known total of individuals to about 100 at several sites. Both locations are still kept secret, yet some bushwalkers are known to have somehow made their way there – illegally and thoughtlessly. Despite stringent disinfection procedures to avoid diseases being brought into the sites on visitors' feet, at least some of the trees have been infected with a rampant fungal disease. Anti-fungal treatments have had to be administered as a result.

The first Wollemi pine planted in public (centre left) had to be protected from souvenir hunters

It now seems likely that the Wollemi pine once grew across much of eastern Australia and may have ranged even further across the ancient supercontinent of Gondwana, embracing Antarctica, New Zealand and possibly India and South America. Its ancestors seem to have been around for a vast span of time, possibly going back 200 million years, and were still reasonably common as little as two million years ago. It is clear that the Wollemi pine is closely related to other Australian pines, notably the kauri, Norfolk Island, hoop and bunya pines, as well as monkey-puzzle pines elsewhere.

The lifespan of the trees themselves is something of a mystery. Dating of cross-sections from the fallen trunk of a 40-metre tree suggests it is about 350 years old. These trees can sprout new trunks by coppicing, however, so the age of a single trunk may be far less than that of the genetic individual, which could have a root system that is many centuries older. Four or five trunks are not uncommon for a single tree. Remarkably, these pines have little or no detectable genetic variation between them. They are deeply inbred yet, being bisexual, they can still produce viable seed. Like the Mongarlowe Mallee, it would seem that the world changed around this species and it went into a long slow decline when the world plunged into a series of ice ages from about two million years ago. Its relic populations must have become so isolated from each other that cross-fertilisation between them became physically impossible. Only those with the capacity to reproduce asexually – in this case by cloning – were able to survive in places like these few canyons, where conditions suited them perfectly.

A few years after their discovery, I was fortunate to visit Cathy Offord, a Royal Botanic Gardens researcher who was studying their reproduction. I was amazed to see scores of young Wollemi pines growing vigorously in greenhouses at the Mount Annan research facility, south-west of Sydney. These were from cuttings and Offord was impressed by how happily the pines had taken to life in a plastic pot. They have proved to be highly amenable to a wide range of growing conditions and temperatures, which is not what might have been expected. In her laboratory, Offord showed me under a microscope an actual embryo of one of the seeds, a pale white little thing that I

Tree business

Call me churlish but these days I feel far less sentimental about the Wollemi pine. In October 2005, I found myself in the Royal Botanic Gardens entering a fenced enclosure dubbed the Wollemi Pine Wilderness, which I was promised was 'recreating the magic' of the secret grove in which the parent trees grow. In fact, I found a thrown-together auction venue, an outdoor viewing room surrounded by wire fencing. Rows of young Wollemi pines were assembled there, their bases covered with mulch to hide their black plastic pots, and labelled with lot numbers.

The Sotheby's catalogue for a forthcoming auction of almost 300 of what were dubbed the 'first generation Collector's Edition' Wollemi pines was a glossy pitch asking thousands of dollars for each of these trees to be offered for open public sale. Each 'lot' was numbered and its lineage linked to its parent tree in the wild dubbed with twee names like the Gaia, the Linnaeus and Hercules. Well, duh, as they say. If each tree in the wild is genetically identical, I wondered, what difference would it make which one the cutting came from? And wouldn't the same be true for the thousands of other clones being grown by the latest high-tech methods for retail sale by Wollemi Australia (a joint venture between a commercial nursery and Queensland's Department of Primary Industries)?

My scepticism was clearly not shared by the eager buyers who parted with more than $1 million to snap up the entire offering. Now, your local nursery has them available for sale as well, the result of a concerted and deliberate effort to commercialise the Wollemi pine after its discovery. Don't get me wrong: with so many Wollemi pines in existence – and the demand to buy one is international – the future of this incredible species will be assured. It's a legitimate conservation strategy. No bushfire, storm, drought or disease could possibly kill every one of them. Before long they'll be growing all over the place, and why not? They're handsome trees and their tale of survival is a wonder and a joy. What's more, a share of the profits will go back into research and conservation of these and other important plants.

As I see it, though, three-quarters of all Australia's plants are unique to this continent. We have botanical riches galore that are all but ignored and barely explored for their commercial, food, medicinal, industrial, environmental and cultural potential. We have historic trees – like the Bennelong Twins that stood barely a kilometre away from the Wollemi pine auction – that don't even rate the faintest blip on our radar. I'm thrilled and delighted that the Wollemi pine has become a household name and that its capacity to generate interest and excitement has infected so many people. But I can't understand why we heap so much praise and expectation on just one tree and leave so many others to their fate.

found quite touching to see. Here was the very essence of life, much like the tiny buds of cells that lead eventually to people. I had never felt such a sense of bondage between plants and animals before.

The scientists did their work well and we are all fortunate that the tree proved relatively easy to propagate and, surprisingly perhaps, adaptable to a wide range of growing conditions. The distribution of specimens to botanic gardens around the world and its successful commercialisation for public sale will ensure that its future is far more secure.

I raise a toast to the Wollemi pine, for its own sake and in the hope that the public passion for this tree will be the spearhead for us to renew our acquaintance with the many others that merit our attention and care. Another way of doing so – and still turn a dollar out of them – is to keep our crown jewels just as they are and give people the opportunity to experience them first-hand. Tourists are voting with the feet, for example, to visit private and public forest walks, in particular, and the small but growing number of elevated boardwalks.

Tree Walks

In the incredible Valley of the Giants, near Walpole in Western Australia's south coast, the excellent Ancient Empire boardwalk takes you to – and, in one case, right through the middle of – the most magical old red tingle trees. One of these rare and beautiful trees has a trunk sixteen metres in diameter (another elsewhere has been measured at 22.3 metres). Next door is the Tree Tops Walk, another elevated walkway that whisks you up into the tops of towering karri trees. I can vouch that standing 40 metres above the forest floor, watching birds fly below you and hearing the wind sing in the crowns of these mighty gums, is more than worth the modest admission price. Many, many other tourists before me and since would agree.

The spectacular Tahune Forest Airwalk in Tasmania, for example, takes visitors on a 600-metre stroll, twenty metres above the ground among the treetops. The highlight is a breathtaking view of the forests and the junction of the Picton and Huon Rivers as you stand on a cantilevered perch 48 metres above the water.

The 600-metre walkway is a cleverly designed series of 60-metre lightweight steel trusses built on steel pylons. It was built to stop this special forest being loved to death by tramping feet. When it opened in 1996, it had cost $1.8 million to build. By the time you read this, some 1.8 million people will have walked over it, gasping and wide-eyed, and it will have paid for itself many times over. In years to come, tourism will generate many times the timber value of these forests if they had been cut down, and many times the jobs. There's a lesson there somewhere.

King's Holly:
Oldest living tree on earth

SOUTH-WEST TASMANIA

No tree – of any kind, anywhere – impresses me more than King's Holly. It is, without question, Australia's greatest tree. That's a big rap and right now you're probably asking yourself 'King's what? If it's our greatest tree, why haven't I heard of it?' Good question, and I wish I knew the answer. While rival trees have achieved international stardom, this truly outstanding one has languished undeservedly on the publicity B-list.

What is greatness? It's whatever we say it is, so long as the term is used to denote something well beyond the ordinary, exceptional or remarkable. Rod Laver is one of the greats of tennis, the Great Australian Bight is indeed a bloody big bight and the great white shark is exactly that.

King's Holly is the greatest of the great because it alone can lay claim to be the world's oldest living tree. It is a genuine freak of nature, a titleholder that blows away other contenders for the crown. Since great longevity is one of the two distinguishing traits of trees (the other being great size) it is a special crown indeed.

For many years North America's bristlecone pine was thought to be the longest-lived tree. These wonderful trees grow on windswept mountaintops, acquiring fascinatingly grotesque shapes in the process. They still hold the record for the most annual growth rings of any tree; one known as Prometheus that once grew in Nevada had 4862 of them. A creosote bush in the Mojave Desert is estimated to be 12 000 years old and a North American huckleberry is thought to be about 13 000 years – a rival to the Mongarlowe Mallee.

King's Holly, however, goes far beyond all of them. To look at it, you would never guess. It grows in south-west Tasmania, in only one gully at the foothills of the Bathurst Range, not far from the coast at Cox Blight. A few hundred stems of the tree are spread over about a kilometre of the gully, scattered among rainforest relics on the edges of several creeks and surrounded by buttongrass plains.

Its highly restricted range makes it especially vulnerable to harm from fires, human disturbance or accidental introductions of disease, so its exact location is a closely guarded secret. It's a small tree with distinctive shiny dark-green leaves that remind me more of a grevillea than holly. It is not a holly at all, but a lomatia (*Lomatia tasmanica*), of which Tasmania has two other species; they are members of the protea family. King's Holly produces pretty sprays of crimson flowers, which also bear a passing resemblance to those of some grevilleas.

Its trunks, best described as stems, rise no higher than about eight metres tall and are very slender. Although they don't come much thicker than a wine bottle, looks are deceptive because they grow very slowly. A growth-ring count found that one stem a mere two centimetres thick – not much fatter than a man's thumb – was about 60 years old. Another stem about seven centimetres thick boasted 240 growth rings, meaning that it started growing before European settlement of Australia.

Recognition that this plant was special was a long time coming. Credit for its discovery goes to Charles Denison King (1909–91), a great Tasmanian bushman whose colourful story is lovingly told by Christobel Mattingley in *King of the Wilderness: the Life of Deny King*.

A man with a hunger for natural history and a meticulous observer, King had an encyclopaedic knowledge of the plants and animals of the Huon Valley

Unsung hero and freak of nature: King's Holly

and Lake Pedder regions and was a valued and trusted collector for museums and scientists. Mattingley records that King had a long and fruitful collaboration with Winifred Curtis, a botanist at the University of Tasmania. Curtis wrote to King in 1965 about her special interest in several plants that he had collected. Among the beautifully pressed flowers was a plant King had first found in 1937 in just one location and now he had found it again, about five kilometres away. Curtis wrote to him about it, wondering whether it was a lomatia previously unknown to science: 'I am most anxious to have fruits of this plant (and of course, any more flowering material in due season!).

King obliged by undertaking an arduous walk to the site, where he prised up six suckers and cut a section of the wood. Their arrival caused a stir among Curtis's

Old, older ... oldest?

colleagues, even more so when King returned to the site the following year and managed to collect samples of its crimson flowers. Curtis was now able to confirm that this small, rare tree was indeed a new species of lomatia. King's discovery is commemorated in its common name, King's Holly.

The first population found by King in 1937 has since disappeared, apparently destroyed by fire, so it was concern for the remaining stand that took researchers from Hobart's Royal Botanical Gardens to the site in the mid-1990s, with special permission to collect four specimens to propagate. Try as they might, however, they could not get cuttings to grow. What's more, although the trees flowered they never bore fruit or produced seeds.

It wasn't until 1998, when University of Tasmania researchers performed genetic tests, that it was realised that all four plants were genetically identical. What's more, the wild ones were identical as well. King's Holly, it emerged, was not a single population but a single individual, spreading underground via its roots and sending up new shoots as it went. It wasn't a colony of runts at all, but one huge genetic individual – a botanical Medusa with many heads. The realisation dawned that for such a slow-growing tree to have spread over such a great area, it must be very old indeed.

But the surprises didn't stop there. The genetic studies revealed that instead of the usual pairs of chromosomes that carry genes, its chromosomes came in threes. During reproduction, chromosome pairs usually split and team up with a new partner but, being triploid, that could never happen with King's Holly: it was sterile. So, that explained why it never bore fruit and why there was only one of them.

The real stunner, though, was the thought that Deny King had first collected other specimens five kilometres away. This plant had clearly been alive for much longer than its present spread would suggest. No one can be sure of the plant's exact age. But fossilised leaves identical to those of the living tree were found in swampy sediments nearby. Since the species cannot reproduce sexually, they must be from the very same plant. Those fossils have been carbon-dated at a minimum age of 43 000 years. The scientists who performed the tests put the upper age limit of the fossils at 130 000 years.

That makes King's Holly the world's most outstanding survivor – apart from some bacteria, no other plant or animal has endured for so long. It is a truly awesome feat that took this little tree through the deep freeze of the last Ice Age, weathering countless storms, floods, fires and droughts. If it is as much as 130 000 years old, it has been growing continuously since about the time that anatomically modern *Homo sapiens* first evolved in Africa, the whole of human history.

With such powers of longevity you'd think King's Holly would be a breeze to grow but, ten years of scientific effort has been met by frustration after frustration. Its propensity to self-cloning has been no help either. Stem cuttings, leaf cuttings and grafts onto closely related plants have all been tried to no avail.

When I visited the research team in the Hobart Royal Botanic Gardens to see the plant, the trays of glossy green frond-like leaves and shoots taking root in the greenhouse attested to the fact that they thrive initially, but beyond that stage it all goes wrong. The young leaves soon blacken, wither and die. Of the four wild stems they collected, only one is still alive. Its growth has been stunted by all the cuttings taken from it.

'It's amazing to me that it's lived so long,' says Natalie Papworth, the botanist charged with trying to coax out the secret of its success. 'But the problem with growing them is that every time we move them or re-pot them they turn up their toes.'

Her colleague Alan Macfadyen wonders whether the problem lies with missing soil microbes that may have a symbiotic relationship with the tree. Some key ingredient from its recipe for success seems to be missing.

'It's certainly getting to the stage where something will have to be done,' Papworth says. 'It has real problems and it is very picky. We may have better success with root cuttings but the problem is we have so few plants we're loathe to dig them up for their roots.' The team next plans to go a bit more high-tech, using artificial tissue-culture techniques to emulate what the plant itself learned to do so very long ago. If King's Holly can teach us anything, it is the inestimable value of patience and persistence. One day its star will shine and this international treasure will get the attention it deserves.

Old, older . . . oldest?

Big, bigger . . .
biggest?

The Monkira Monster

MONKIRA STATION, QUEENSLAND

Its name seems more suited to a bloodthirsty beast from a horror movie. But the amazing Monkira Monster is a truly exceptional whopper of a tree that for sheer size alone demands inclusion in this book. It is indeed a monster, one of the mightiest eucalypts ever known. What's more, it's a coolibah that has camped itself by a billabong. And grows in Queensland, where another coolibah – plus a local yarn about a sheep-stealing swaggie who drowned in a waterhole while fleeing the law – inspired a young poet named A.B. (Banjo) Paterson in 1895 to write the lyrics of 'Waltzing Matilda'.

While no Aussies worth their salt could be unfamiliar with that famous song, our increasingly urban lives mean that few of us today would be able to recognise a coolibah tree. Fewer still would have heard of the Monkira Monster. Despite its unique stature, it is the forgotten colossus of Australian trees. I knew nothing about it until I was researching this book and by chance found a reference to it in a little 1964 publication called *Tree Wonders of Australia*, by A.E. Brooks. It contained no photograph of the tree but it did say:

> It grows near the Neuragully Waterhole in far-western Queensland. The distance around the tree is given as 250 yards, the height as 60 feet and the distance around the trunk as 46 feet. As the lower part of the trunk is buried beneath a few yards of silt, it may well be that, nearer to the roots, the girth would be much greater. From the trunk of this tree which is known as the Monkira Monster, a maze of large, twisted, ugly branches grows outward for distances of up to about 120 feet. This could easily be Australia's most spreading tree.

Facing page: The Monster: one of the few pictures of it, taken in 2001

After searching high and low for more information I could only find a similarly brief reference to it in a 1963 *Australian Encyclopaedia*, which described it as 'probably the largest example of its species ever known'. It additionally gave the tree's height as 'about 100 feet'.

It wasn't until I converted all the imperial measurements into metric that I realised with a shock that the tree was even larger than I had first comprehended. I tried to picture it in my head. It was 30 metres tall and the visible part of the trunk was fourteen metres around. It would take seven adults joining hands to encircle it. Measured from the trunk, the longest branches reached out almost 37 metres, the length of three cricket pitches. But it was the size of the circle traced by its foliage that left me speechless: 750 feet is about 228 metres. If you lowered a measuring tape to the ground from the roof of Sydney's MLC Centre – at 65 storeys high, it was once the tallest building in Australia – that's the same length of tape you'd need to measure a walk around the outer limits of this tree. Apart from these two sources, however, I could find no further information about the Monster. I assumed that, like so many other valuable heritage trees, this one must have died.

Later, while trolling through the National Library of Australia's picture collection, I came across some old black-and-white photographs taken by Arthur Groom, a notable photographer, author and conservationist. He had visited Monkira Station in 1952, when a pedal wireless was still used to communicate with the outside world. One of Groom's photographs depicted a near-treeless plain with several young stockmen on horseback. Another showed three men posing stiffly for the camera near a pitched tent in a stock camp, with a pile of cut timber for firewood: the men appeared to be from successive generations and the eldest wore a jacket and hat. He must have been remarkable in his own right, because the picture was captioned: 'Don McKenzie, the Monkira head-stockman on the left is over 80 years old.'

But it was the caption on the third picture in the series that made me gasp: 'Mr Bob Gunther, manager of Monkira, and the giant coolibah, 46 feet around the girth.' There it was, the Monkira Monster! It showed a middle-aged man sitting cross-legged on a low limb – it must have been a metre thick – of a whopping great tree. A massively broad trunk covered in deeply cracked and furrowed bark; great sprawling branches jutting off at all angles; and hollows where earlier limbs had long-since broken off and decayed. Not only was this tree very large but it was also clearly very old, even then.

This was a marvellous find. But surely if such a tree were still alive today it would be famous, mentioned regularly in dispatches when important trees were in the public eye? Even allowing for the fact that Monkira Station is well off the beaten track, 130 kilometres east of Bedourie in the remote Channel Country of far-western Queensland,

you would assume a natural wonder like this would be noted often enough by the small army of four-wheel-drive nomads who now ply the byways and backblocks of the land in growing numbers.

I searched no more for the Monster and got on with the rest of this book. In the final stages of writing, though, I came across my notes about it and thought I should try to resolve the mystery of what had happened to it.

Assuming the worst, I telephoned Monkira Station to find out when the tree had died and whether a stump, memorial or even some small souvenir of its wood was left. The manager, Anthony Desereaux, listened politely to my questions and said: 'Yes, I know about that tree. But you'd do better to speak with my wife Debbie; she takes much more interest in history and that sort of thing.' That confirmed it: the tree literally was history, I thought.

But my spirits soared when she came on the line and broke the good news: the Monster was still there, and alive! Debbie explained that she had visited the tree often in their four years at Monkira. 'It is an amazing tree,' she said. 'It grows right on the edge of the waterhole and it is very old.' It is still made of sturdy stuff. When rains flood the Channel Country, the Neuragully Waterhole fills and submerges the Monster's trunk several metres deep. Conversely, in the last big drought in 2002 the waterhole dried up completely, Debbie recalls.

The tree has not been measured for some time, so its current dimensions are unknown. They almost certainly have changed in the 50 years since those last written records of it. We don't know how old it is, either, but if it was so large in 1952 it must already have seen centuries pass. Coolibahs can certainly be long-lived: a veteran specimen at Hughenden carries the blaze marks of two expeditions from the 1860s, both in search of Burke and Wills.

How is it, I asked Debbie, that so little attention is paid to the tree by the outside world? She has wondered that herself although, as she explains, it is not signposted and is not accessible by public road. The Desereauxs greatly admire the tree and, because of its age and vulnerability to damage, they are careful to vet those who seek access to the property for camping and hunting. Any reader wanting to see it must make a personal approach to the station management for permission to do so. Happily, in recent years the waterhole and the tree have been fully fenced off from cattle under the Land for Wildlife scheme, with part of the fencing cost supported by the Federal Government's Envirofund. The fence is ten kilometres long and is set back from the water by a minimum of 500 metres. Regeneration of the billabong banks and floodplain is expected to follow,

Debbie Desereaux and young friends with the Monster in 2006

stabilising the soil and attracting back wildlife. Many other small coolibahs grow near to the Monster, and Debbie suspects it is the parent tree.

It has certainly witnessed great changes in its time. The region was settled by pastoralists in the 1880s. Monkira is on the Diamantina River and belongs to NAPCO – the privately owned North Australian Pastoral Company – one of the largest cattle producers in Australia. The station sprawls over hundreds of thousands of hectares of land that is flooded with a crisscross network of rivers, creeks and watercourses after rain. Although dry seasons can be harsh, the region ranks among the best cattle fattening country in Australia. Monkira is famous for producing another monster in the 1890s: a shorthorn bullock raised there, known as the Monkira Ox, weighed an impressive 1381 kilograms.

The tallest trees

The tallest living tree species in Australia are all eucalypts. The top seven, measured by laser, are listed below with their world ranking in brackets:

1. Mountain ash, *E. regnans* 97.0m (3rd)
2. Tasmanian blue gum, *E. globulus* 90.7m (6th)
3. Manna gum, *E. viminalis* 88.9m (8th)
4. Alpine ash, *E. delegatensis* 87.9m (10th)
5. Messmate stringybark, *E. obliqua* 84.8m (12th)
6. Shining gum, *E. nitens* 84.3m (13th)
7. Karri, *E. diversicolor* 80.5m (17th)

The Deseraux family lives in the station homestead. Fire damage in the 1970s revealed 60-centimetre-thick sandstone walls from its original core. In those tough early times disease took its toll. Among a number of pioneer-era graves on the station are four belonging to young stockmen, who were only in their late teens or early twenties when they lost their lives to typhoid fever.

The late Bob Gunther, the man in that 1952 photograph, managed the station for many years and is well remembered. His initials are still visible where he carved them in an old fencepost. Debbie also found his initials scratched into an old bottle that she salvaged and made sure to pass on to Gunther's son. Even though few of us will ever see it for ourselves, the Monkira Monster is in good hands.

Groom's 1952 photo of Monkira men: Don McKenzie, head stockman (left) was over 80 years old

The King of the Eucalypts
TASMANIA AND VICTORIA

'It is recorded that two expert axemen, working on a platform 15 feet above the ground, took two and a half days to cut a scarf 6 feet deep into the mighty butt as a preliminary to sending the giant toppling to earth. The crash of its fall sounded for miles around and even hardened bushworkers are said to have downed tools in silent homage to the fallen monarch. Its age was put at 400 years and it was calculated that when Abel Tasman discovered the island in 1642 this tree was already a noble specimen of between 150 and 200 feet in height.'

This giant mountain ash from the Derwent Valley was later pulped into 75 tons of newsprint.

Alexander Rule

The mountain ash is a simply stupendous tree. But it often doesn't seem so at first. If you stand beneath a healthy young one and follow its slim cylindrical trunk upwards with your eye, past a hanging tangled mass of tightly curled bark sheddings, you see something best described as a giant toothpick with a bit of green fairy floss on top. This beanpole of the bush is not especially attractive, at least not until it gets into its dotage and its base takes on the bulky, buttressed, mossy charm of the other great denizens of the wet south-eastern forests. It's a great streak of a thing – messy in its habits, ungainly in its branch patterns, inclined to lose its head in high winds and to rot in its middle. But in their old age they are a wonderful, inspiring, humbling sight, cloaked in antiquity and often decked in a green velvet covering of moss and lichens.

It can be hard to take in the sight of one as an individual tree because of their

tendency to grow en masse, like close-packed ranks of stilt-walkers standing to attention. For the same reason they can be wretchedly hard to photograph. It's not until you start absorbing the vital statistics about how tall they can grow, and how fast, that you come to appreciate why this is the king of the eucalypts, the undisputed grand champion of its kind.

First the bare facts. Mountain ash – known unflatteringly in Tasmania as swamp gum – grows in the wet open forests of the Otway Ranges in southern Victoria in the Gippsland region in eastern Victoria and in north-eastern and southern Tasmania. As it matures it sheds its lower branches and, in classic gum-tree style, develops a columnar white or grey trunk, usually bare of bark except near the ground. It occurs from sea level to altitudes over 1000 metres. It is fire-sensitive and relies on seed for regeneration. It is a significant tree commercially, providing both logs and pulp, if nothing else because of its sheer size. One mountain ash yields a lot of wood and its trunk may be clean-barrelled (bare of branches) for 60 or more metres from the ground. That fact alone was one of its major attractions to early woodcutters with only hand tools available to fell and trim them.

Perhaps as a result of its capacity to grow very fast and very tall, it does not reach an immense age. Nevertheless, its life expectancy exceeds 400 years, equivalent to about sixteen human generations. The oldest mountain ash trees alive in Australia today were strapping young things in 1642, when Abel Tasman headed for the South Seas. They had seen two centuries of life before the First Fleet arrived in Sydney Harbour.

Mountain ash forest in Victoria, a cathedral of beauty

Older specimens develop massive buttressed bases but – like most eucalypts – the bole does not usually remain thick for very far up the tree. Woodcutters noted in olden times that a big mature one could have a diameter of six metres at chest height but they thinned rapidly to only two metres once you got a few metres higher. That's why those old pictures of tree fellers show them standing on springboards well off the ground.

The broadest living mountain ash today probably doesn't exceed four or five metres in diameter at chest height but some real whoppers were measured and

Big, bigger . . . biggest?

recorded a century or more ago. One of the largest was the King Edward VII Tree, that grew in scenic mountain country near Marysville, about 75 kilometres north-east of Melbourne. Its vital statistics were taken by a licensed surveyor: at ground level it was almost eleven metres in diameter. As happened to so many other massive old trees and tree stumps, a series of bushfires in the 1920s destroyed all trace of the King Edward VII Tree.

In South Gippsland, the Bulga Stump – all that remained of that tree at the time – was measured at 10.8 metres in diameter at chest height before it was engulfed by fire in 1890. Many other mighty Victorian mountain ash trees – such as the Mueller or Furmston Tree at Mount Monda, the massive Horsfall Tree on the Toorongo Plateau and the regal 99-metre-tall Neerim Giant at Neerim – survived the rapacious loggers only to perish in bushfires. None lasted beyond 1939.

Several other trees in Victoria were reportedly broader still, but the largest reliable measurement I was able to track down was from Tasmania. An unnamed tree measured in the nineteenth century at the foot of Mount Wellington, near Hobart, had a base diameter of 12.6 metres. When people walked along the corpse of the fallen tree they found that it had lost its top: at that break point, 67 metres from its base, the trunk was still an amazing 3.7 metres in diameter – absolutely huge.

El Grande: Australia's largest tree
FLORENTINE VALLEY, TASMANIA

It was a chilly winter's Sunday when Wally Herrmann ushered his terrier dog Toby McTrouble into his car and headed out of Hobart into the wild green forests of Tasmania. They were going in search of giants. Giant trees, that is. As it turned out, they found one – a real beauty – just in time to save its life. But there the fairytale ended. This is his account of the truly tragic, dumb and totally preventable fate that befell Australia's largest tree, El Grande. It is an object lesson and a stark reminder that, no matter how big or small they are, trees are living things.

Acting on a tip-off, Wally and McTrouble headed straight for the Florentine Valley, a cold-climate rainforest in Central Tasmania, near Wayatinah, only two hours' drive from the busy streets of the state capital. In this extraordinary valley the mountain ash trees have found a place that suits them well – soil, water, aspect and temperature –to grow not only tall but sometimes fat and bulky, too.

Forests like these in Tasmania have truly stood the test of time. The biggest mountain ashes live for centuries. If you could fast-forward a film of its life and times you would see the forest progress through stages. The process is usually kick-started when a hot bushfire sweeps through a valley and kills the standing trees. Big as they are, not even they can withstand the intense heat. They rely on shedding millions upon millions of their tiny seeds into the carbon-rich debris of the fire to replace themselves. Enterprising wattles get in first and rapidly colonise, stabilising the bare ground. They usually dominate for a couple of decades, seizing their days in the sun. But soon the slender young eucalypt saplings poke their heads above the wattles and start to overshadow them. The dimmer, less exposed conditions beneath the gums and wattles allow the rise of the shade-tolerant rainforest species with lyrical names

– sassafras, myrtle beech, celery-top and tree ferns – to eventually form a dense canopy about 30 metres high.

This canopy steals so much light that the wattles fade away, relegated to the fringes and clearings of the forest. It also halts the recruitment of new mountain ash seedlings. The gums are outnumbered by other tree species, but the survivors respond to the competition by growing taller still. After a couple of centuries, only the tall pioneer gums poke out from the canopy, typically reaching up 60 metres. After four centuries or so, they gradually disintegrate from the top down and fall, leaving other species to take the rainforest on to its climax stage, which can persist for centuries more until the next fire.

Herrmann, a senior geologist at the University of Tasmania and a longtime conservationist, loves forests such as these. He is a passionate observer of the finest specimens among them and has spent many, many hours searching for them. He went to Wayatinah on 9 June 2002 to scout for the Wilderness Society – of which he is a member – after it heard reports that Forestry Tasmania was harvesting some very large logs from rainforests there. The society particularly wanted Herrmann to check whether any remaining trees came under FT's tall-trees policy, which aimed to spare the rare specimens over 85 metres tall. His hope was that if he could find any, the logging might be stopped. Armed with maps, extensive bushwalking and exploration experience, a borrowed laser rangefinder for measuring tree heights, a Thermos of tea and biscuits for McTrouble, he followed rough forestry roads until he reached the coupe where it was thought such trees might be. But it had been clearfelled some years earlier and was now a plantation of gum saplings.

Man and dog spent several hours exploring further, Herrmann roughly mapping out extensive cleared and regrowth areas and estimating heights of trees in remnant patches of tall forest. None was more than 60 metres and there had been no recent forestry activity. By mid-afternoon he was feeling discouraged, having seen only cleared areas, young regrowth or unremarkable remnant patches of forest.

Then he came across the wheel marks of heavy vehicles on a spur road and followed them until he reached the edge of a recently cleared slope. There were piles of green logs, machinery parked near a loading bay and a small sign at the roadside indicating that logging was in progress – coupe CO 004E – although, being the Queen's Birthday holiday weekend, no work was in progress. Hermann recalled the scene:

> A newly clearfelled old-growth rainforest coupe is a grim scene and not easy to traverse. It's a nimble effort to clamber through the tangled masses of downed tree trunks and branches, tree ferns, stumps and churned-up ground.

Wally Hermann poses at the massive base of the tree

McTrouble and I slipped and scrambled up the muddy snig tracks from the log landing and over slash-piles into a sleety south-westerly wind, suitably bleak, through the tragic devastation. A group of tall trees – mountain ash – standing at the very western edge of the clearing against the backdrop of undisturbed ancient forest, seemed to draw us uphill towards them.

One gum with a massive buttressed trunk stood apart from the others, about ten metres from the edge of the standing rainforest. Understorey plants, ferns and smaller trees had been cleared away or flattened around it, and some large cut stumps and discarded hollow butts were nearby. It seemed that this big fellow would be one of the next trees to go.

Its exposure at the edge of the clearfell seemed to enhance its stature. I ran the tape measure around, made some observations for height, took photographs, and realised it was the biggest stem I'd ever seen in Tasmania – just over 80 metres tall, with a girth of 19.7 metres at shoulder height. Awesome as the tree was, that realisation didn't have much immediate impact. I was thinking how sad it was that in a couple of days, such a magnificent, ancient being would be cut down, dismembered, sliced into short lengths and carted unceremoniously off to the saw or, still worse, the chipper. Furthermore, we were searching for trees over 85 metres tall – that being Forestry Tasmania's self-determined threshold for protection of giant trees – and its massive girth was not a recognised criterion.

Herrmann measured some nearby trees between 70 and 75 metres tall then made a circuit through the standing forest to the west. Judging by the forest structure, he guessed that it had not seen a bushfire for at least 300 years. These were fairytale places – the big gum trees, the rainforest understorey of myrtle beech, sassafras and celery-top – and beautiful to the eye with the ferns and green mosses all over the ground.

With the sun sinking low, he returned to the clearfell and sat on a fresh-cut giant stump while Toby ate the last of his dog biscuits and he finished his tea and made notes in his field book. Before leaving, he briefly gazed at the massive tree again, one of the small leafy branches at its top streaming out like a pennant in the bitter wind.

Back in Hobart, Herrmann telephoned Steve Whitely, Forestry Tasmania's manager for the Derwent District, and told him about the big tree. 'I was fully expecting to be told to nick off and leave forest harvesting plans to the foresters. But the response was magnanimous: Steve agreed that this tree could be significant and said he'd send someone out the next day to measure it.' FT decided to stop logging on the coupe and placed a machine exclusion zone around the big tree while its soundness and size were assessed. FT soon issued a media release, in which it claimed to have measured the tree two years earlier but decided it did not merit protection because it was below the 85-metre threshold. Now, FT said, it was developing a more inclusive protection policy that recognised trees of massive volume as well. It measured Herrmann's giant as 79 metres tall and 18.7 metres in girth, possibly exceeding in volume the previous record holder, the Arve Big Tree, which is 87 metres tall, 17.1 metres in girth and 404 cubic metres in volume.

'I had seen the Arve Big Tree but hadn't known its dimensions,' Herrmann says. 'It then began to dawn on me that the CO 004E giant might not merely be the biggest tree I'd seen – it could be the most massive in the State.' Indeed it was. It was also the largest living tree in Australia and, all things considered, outstanding globally by any standard.

Herrmann spent many more weekends through to the summer of 2003 searching for other giants, mainly on about fifteen planned coupes in the contentious Styx Valley.

'Tree searching is enjoyable: it's a peaceful and yet exciting exploratory quest; it's connected me with great forests and some good people,' he says. FT even helped him a little for pragmatic reasons, providing maps to narrow down the search. But by the end of January, he'd found no more official tall trees and only one that might qualify as an official giant by volume. Worse, from his point of view, the temporary protection of the remainder of the coupe and its giant tree had hastened the clearfelling of other big trees nearby.

Still, by late 2002, the FT protection policy was broadened to preclude cutting any trees with a stem volume exceeding 280 cubic metres. When a list of Tasmania's '10 most massive giants' appeared on FT's website, at the top of the list was the CO 004E tree at 439 cubic metres — 35 cubic metres more than the Arve Big Tree and 110 cubic metres clear of the third-largest. Herrmann's giant was listed as number TT85 in the FT tall trees database, and had somehow been dubbed El Grande. Herrmann doesn't like the name: El Tragico would better reflect its subsequent fate, he says.

In January 2003, FT put out another media release saying that old age was catching up with El Grande; it was 'over-mature', highly decayed, its base was 80 per cent hollow — at one point, coring tools penetrated only 8 centimetres of solid wood before hitting decayed wood – and was nearing the end of its life. A reserve would be placed around the tree, which was 'prone to breakage' but 'could remain standing for some years to come'. Seeds had been collected from it and the surrounding area would be 'regenerated back to native forest, including swamp gums that will grow into tall trees for future generations'.

The media release also estimated for the first time that El Grande was about 350 years old. That meant it had germinated around the time Abel Tasman 'discovered' Tasmania in 1642. It was still a small seedling when New York was not yet even a named colony and Wall Street owed its name to fortifications built against the English, when the Dutch were first settling Cape Town and when Cromwell was seeing off King Charles I. It had lived its youth through and beyond the industrial revolution; its middle age easily exceeded the whole of Queen Victoria's reign; it endured the rise and rise of the car, the age of powered flight, countless wars, depressions, volcanoes, earthquakes, the atomic age, the space age and the computer age: in short, it had stood firm through the entire modern history of Australia.

Herrmann returned to the tree in early March to show it to Ronnie Harrison, a self-described American 'big-tree hunter' who had enthusiastically come all the way from his home in Texas after hearing about El Grande in news reports. 'We were dismayed to find that some idiot and a big earthmoving machine had swept clear a circular area immediately around the base of the tree, tearing up some of its shallow

Facing page: Before and after: El Grande did not survive the fire

roots, in clear violation of the 100-metre machinery exclusion zone proclaimed by FT, and certainly not improving its chance of survival,' Herrmann says.

The bare ground was parched dry and dead vegetation crackled under foot. They photographed the scene but then – to his ongoing regret – Herrmann was laid low by a painful illness for a month and wasn't able to lodge a protest as he intended. On 15 April, Whitely telephoned him with the news that a 'regeneration' fire on the cleared part of coupe CO 004E had slightly singed El Grande – a bit of bark, some dead leaves, but no serious harm done. 'Hmm,' Herrmann said, 'that's pretty careless – why did you have to burn the coupe and why didn't you have adequate firefighting gear on site to control the fire?' Herrmann found it hard to understand how a fire could have reached the tree, given that the ground around it had been cleared. A stray spark or two could not have done it and would have been easily extinguishable.

The same day, an FT media release headed 'Florentine giant stands tall' quoted Whitely as saying that El Grande had 'once again demonstrated the natural resilience eucalypts have to fire'. It also conceded that despite efforts to protect it – by clearing away debris, forming firebreaks and wetting the trunk – a regeneration burn had 'impacted' on it, charring the trunk and lower inside portion. It was expected to 'shed its current covering of leaves before new leaves begin to shoot'. There was an air of confidence in this: 'We will be conducting a review of the condition of El Grande with a professional arborist in the near future to best manage its future.' It later explained:

> Forestry Tasmania's local District staff conducted a regeneration burn at the coupe containing El Grande to prepare the 30-hectare site for regeneration back to native forest. Harvesting residues were burnt to also reduce the risk of any wildfire spreading into adjoining forest areas. Despite the fact that firebreaks were constructed and the big tree was wetted-down, sparks from the fire caught into dry branches and caused a hot burn around the tree, setting it alight.

A day later, Herrmann had another phone call about El Grande, from an angry and distressed Victorian giant-tree hunter and climber, Brett Mifsud, who had gone with some fellow enthusiasts to climb El Grande to get accurate height and volume estimates. They had arrived there a couple of days after the fire and were shocked to find the coupe completely burnt and the big tree still smoking. Mifsud was livid as he recounted how the fire had caught hold in the fibrous lower bark and gone up the inside of the trunk for many metres before exiting through charred burls and holes higher up. He said the tree had dropped about a third of its crown, including some

Burnt

Like the Tree of Knowledge at Barcaldine, the Shearing Strike Tree, which stood near the Flinders River at Hughenden, was a memorial to the birth of the Labor movement. A large shield-shaped section of bark had been removed from its trunk and on the wood beneath was carved: 'United we stand, Divided we fall. A.L.P. The Strike Camp, 1891.' It was destroyed by fire in 1944.

A worse loss in 1996 was that of Sturt's Tree, which once grew on the banks of the Murray River above Renmark. The 30-metre gum was dead but was much admired for its historic value: not only did it carry alpha-numeric markings – allegedly left by the explorer Charles Sturt (although that claim is in doubt) – but also a massive canoe scar almost nine metres long. It was one of the largest canoe scars known. Tourists moored their houseboat near it and decided to light a campfire on the bank. They failed to notice until too late that the fire had escaped and set the old tree alight. Media reports later said the fire burnt for two days, with the distraught tourists trying fruitlessly all the while to extinguish it.

Another tree, said to have been marked with the word 'Dig' in 1862 by the explorer William Landsborough, was burnt by vandals in 2002 and fell over. That incident sparked a brief frenzy of outrage and dismay in the media, based on the erroneous belief that the original Burke and Wills Dig Tree had been destroyed. The collective sense of loss and grieving we feel after one of these exceptional trees is gone – people literally weep at the news – is sure evidence of the great value we invest in them. Strange then, that we make such a patchy show of conserving, protecting and celebrating them. We could do so much better.

limbs nearly a metre thick, and every leaf on the remainder was brown and crisp.

Herrmann wrote an angry letter to Evan Rolley, FT's managing director, and sent copies to prominent politicians and the editor of the Mercury, but it wasn't published. When Dr Bob Brown, the Greens senator, visited the burnt tree and pronounced it a national disgrace – likening it to blowing up the Sydney Opera House – closer media scrutiny followed. There were calls for an inquiry and the Wilderness Society commissioned an independent expert, consultant botanist Alan Gray, to examine El Grande's health.

Gray reported that the fire 'appears to have been particularly intense in the vicinity of the tree; humus and other organic litter having been burnt to mineral earth'. Tree ferns and smaller shrubs and trees as well as fallen timber were severely charred or destroyed. The removal of 'soil' from around the tree had exposed a number of openings between the buttresses that led to the hollow centre of the tree, a hollow that extended up at least 60 metres. The fire had clearly reached the tree then crept into the ground-level openings, Gray said. Dry rot and wood inside the trunk had ignited and the configuration of draught holes at the base with outlet holes further up – where charring was visible on hollow branches – had acted like a furnace with a chimney. 'The temperatures generated within the tree core must have been extremely high, virtually "cooking" the tree from the inside-out,' Gray reported. Removing some bark to the tree's vital cambium layer revealed dead or near dead tissue. No moisture movement was apparent and 'with the crown of leaves dead (thus no negative pressure to draw sap), the transport systems of this tree must be regarded as defunct'. In short, El Grande was 'clearly dead, from the roots to the crown'.

It was a disaster that made international news. Herrmann says he was later visited by Rolley, who wanted to assure him that he was personally shocked by the accidental torching. 'He said he and FT colleagues had visited El Grande in the previous spring. He'd been very impressed by it and had told his colleagues, "Whatever we do, we must look after this tree", so he was mortified by what had happened.'

In its *Forestry Matters* newsletter in May 2003, FT expressed 'disappointment' about the circumstances of the burn. A national treasure gone without a word of apology. Worse still, the newsletter continued to maintain that there was hope for El Grande, despite obvious and expert evidence to the contrary:

Opinions vary on the health status of the tree. Botanist Alan Gray says the tree is already dead. Other opinion suggests it is too early to be sure either way. What is certain is that the tree's base and significant parts of the interior have been charred. The tree, which stood alone in a harvested area with some understorey shrubs is very old, had dead branches through the crown and showed advanced decay and age. Time alone will tell the story.

What were they thinking? By now they had had time to get an opinion from their own professional arborist. Why make such a statement at that time, when there was no shred of life evident in the poor tree? A terrible, tragic mistake had been made and El Grande clearly was lost. The glare of publicity was intense. FT's competence in forestry was in some doubt, but much more so was its capacity to responsibly manage and conserve the many botanical jewels in its care. Having owned up to its mistake it undid that good immediately by mounting the defence that it wasn't such a bad mistake. This was Australia's largest known tree, for heaven's sake, the biggest, the granddaddy of some 40 billion trees across an entire continent. It had been scorched to a crisp on the outside and roasted alive from the inside.

To its credit, Forestry Tasmania had shown the foresight to collect and store seeds from El Grande, so that its special genes could be carried on to a new generation. No human alive today, of course, will ever see those seedlings reach the proportions of their illustrious forebear.

As part of a forest ecosystem, El Grande probably had no greater significance than many other centuries-old, threatened trees. Herrmann concedes that it was one tree among many. Its loss won't change the world. 'However, it was a mighty lever in shifting human awareness, and I thank it for its huge contribution,' he says. Whatever the future holds for its descendants, questions remain about the quality of FT's stewardship of very large and very tall trees. Self-evidently, trees of such stature are exceedingly rare and in setting the bar so high for protection the policy itself is of dubious merit. What is the point of such a protection policy when so few trees qualify? And, in light of the El Grande tragedy, what good is that 'protection' anyway?

In January 2006, Brett Mifsud returned to Tasmania and anointed El Grande's heir – a 75-metre mountain ash named Two Towers with a volume of 430 cubic metres – Australia's largest living tree.

Trees are indeed living things. They can die slowly or suddenly. El Grande was not the first and it will not be the last to die by fire, accidentally or on purpose. Australia has about 30 'giant' trees that meet the criteria for height and bulk set by Forestry Tasmania. At least thirteen of them are in the Andromeda Reserve: a single fire could thus destroy almost half of the nation's greatest trees. Every time such things happen, we lose another matchless piece of our heritage.

Mountain ash

Dr David Lindenmayer has chronicled the life and times of the ash forests in a beautifully illustrated book, *Life in the Tall Eucalypt Forests*, based on his years of work as a forest ecologist in Victoria's central highlands.

Older mountain ash trees have some special features that make them important members of the forest ecosystem, Lindenmayer says.

Most notably, the number of flowers produced by old-growth individuals is fifteen times greater than in young trees. In some years mountain ash canopies produce particularly large crops of flowers. Exactly what triggers these mass-flowering events is not fully understood but when they occur in old-growth stands they produce huge amounts of nectar and pollen.

The open crowns of older trees also support plenty of mistletoe, the flowers and fruits of which are valuable to birds and mammals. Relatively few individual mountain ash trees can reach great heights because drought periodically stresses them to the point where they can't pump enough water to sustain their crowns. These stag tops can lose ten- to twenty-metre chunks of their antlers at a time through pruning by high winds. The pruning eventually kills the tree, although the process may take 200 years and the corpse of the tree may remain standing for 70 years more. When they, fall their bleached corpses support a whole new food and habitat chain on the forest floor and they can take many more decades to rot and eventually decay.

The hollows that living trees start to accumulate after about 120 years of growth – through attacks by water rot, fungi, bacteria and termites – provide dens for more than 100 species of mammals, birds, reptiles and frogs in a typical mountain ash forest, although far less animal life occupies them in rainforests. The holes and hollows become larger over time and their tenants change as well. Lindenmayer points out that it might take three centuries before the hollows are large enough to suit the mountain brushtail possum. 'The sequential process of tree death and decay in mountain ash creates several distinct "types" of large old trees and the hollows of each of these different tree types are preferred by different animal species.

Sugar gliders and feathertail gliders, for example, prefer nesting in trees with intact crowns, while the greater glider and yellow-bellied glider usually opt to nest in recently dead trees or trees with dead tops. Even a dead tree in advanced decay has its specialist inhabitants. As water, fungi and animal activity rots its centre from the top down, the tree develops an empty centre or 'pipe': the rotten wood and organic debris that accumulates there – colourfully known in forest parlance as mudguts – festers like a compost heap and generates enough warmth to provide a sub-floor heating system to ease the chill on even the coldest days for animals that den there. Even a highly decayed tree consisting of no more than ten metres of piped trunk can be a home for animals such as the rare Leadbeater's possum.

The Ferguson Tree: the tallest tree on earth

WATTS RIVER, VICTORIA

Mountain ash is often called the world's tallest flowering plant. Or sometimes you see it labelled as the world's tallest hardwood. Or the cringe-making 'tallest tree in the Southern Hemisphere'. It is, indeed, all of those things.

That's impressive. But this marvellous Australian tree begs for a much bolder and grander claim to fame. It clearly deserves it: the mountain ash is the world's tallest tree. In fact, I'll go further and say that it is the tallest living thing of any kind, anywhere and at any time, ever, in the history of life on Earth.

Some readers may bristle at this outrageous claim. They could point to the fossil record and demand comparisons over time. While plenty of large fossilised tree trunks have been found, none comes close to those of today. The acknowledged authority on such matters is Dr Al Carder, a Canadian professor of plant science who retired in 1970. Carder spent the next two decades travelling the globe, measuring trees and trolling through scientific papers, journals and official records for information about the world's largest and tallest big trees.

He set out the results in glorious detail in his definitive 1995 book, *Forest Giants of the World: Past and Present*.

Soon after plant life crept from the sea onto the land the advantages of upward growth were accentuated. This, of course, meant expenditure of effort against gravity, but although the cost was considerable the advantages were nearly absolute. Even primitive plants of 300 million years ago were quite successful in this. Some, such as the early forms of clubmoss, rose to 150 feet [45 metres] in height but no species, all through time, ever acquired the complexity of structure or the size of modern trees in the upward thrust for warmth and light.

That takes care of prehistoric contenders.

Readers may also ask how I can ignore the consensus among scientists, foresters and tree buffs everywhere that the current title of the tallest tree is held by the mighty and ancient coast redwood, a North American conifer. That is indeed true, and it's why those who sing the many praises of the Aussie contender have resorted to using lesser titles to single it out for attention.

Records are made to be broken, of course, but the coast redwood's claim to fame is based on the record for the tallest living tree. You don't have to go back far in history – a mere two human lifetimes – to see that the mountain ash was then, by a very large margin, the standout winner. The bad news is that we humans, through a combination of axes and fires, killed off the gold, silver and bronze medallists for the title (along with most of the rest of the contenders). But we're dealing here with plants that live for centuries. The good news is that you probably won't need to live for too much longer to see it regain its title. I certainly hope to before I die.

For now, let's go back to the record books. Until recently, the world's tallest known living tree was a coast redwood – *Sequoia sempervirens* – named the Stratosphere Giant. It was discovered in August 2000 in the Rockefeller Forest of the Humboldt Redwoods State Park, California. Its exact location is not publicised, for the tree's own good. It has grown another 50 centimetres or so since its discovery and, according to *Guinness World Records*, this fabulous plant was officially measured at 112.7 metres tall in July 2004. In 2006, researchers found three redwoods in Redwood National Park that were even taller. The tallest, Hyperion, was 115.5 metres.

Unlike the mountain ash, these trees have vast amounts of time – two millennia or more – in which to reach such dizzying heights. Their habitat also provides copious amounts of water, with annual rainfall of more than 2.5 metres or more, and often a soothing wet fog.

Humboldt has another 25 coast redwoods at or taller than 110 metres. Even larger redwoods were no doubt felled by pioneer axes but none were reliably measured.

Elsewhere in North America historic records point to even taller trees. One Douglas fir – the Lynn Valley tree on North Vancouver Island – was claimed to have reached a formidable 126 metres when measured in 1902. A veteran moss-covered Sitka spruce on Vancouver Island, known as the Carmanah Giant, tops 96 metres. Giant sequoias (*Sequoiadendron giganteum*) of the western Sierra Nevada in California also grow to great heights; the record-holder for that species is said to have been 106 metres. The giant sequoia is far and away the global king of trees in terms of bulk, a tree of such prodigious proportions that no other is ever likely to match it. If you're in Melbourne and would like to see one, there's an attractive young specimen growing in the Royal Botanic Gardens, and Ballarat's gardens have a whole avenue of 28 of them planted from 1863 to 1874.

Many huge trees can be found elsewhere in the world, of course, but rarely do they go much above 60 metres, even in the lush rainforests of South America, Africa and Indonesia. A few individuals growing in particularly favourable conditions have reached about 80 metres (notably the Korean spruce), but the rainforest record more likely goes to the Klinki pine, a species in New Guinea that has reportedly risen to almost 90 metres. Europe has nothing to match this, since even the most ancient oaks and elms rarely trouble the judges beyond 50 metres. The first European settlers to venture into the east coast eucalypt forests must have been staggered by what they found – trees of a height way beyond their prior experience.

It's worth noting, too, that the mountain ash is not the only eucalypt tree to reach great heights. Among those known to top 80 metres are: messmate stringybark (*E. oblique*); alpine ash (*E. delegatensis*); manna gum (*E. viminalis*); and Tasmania's floral emblem, the blue gum (*E. globulus*). One karri, known as Stewarts Karri, near Manjimup in Western Australia, was reportedly measured at 88 metres in 1995. Several species in New South Wales have also been officially measured at well over 75 metres. Specially noteworthy in that state is a stand of fabulous trees in 15 700-hectare Cunnawarra National Park, on the eastern edge of the Northern Tablelands, not far from Armidale. Part of the Central Eastern Rainforest Reserves of Australia World Heritage Area, the northern part of the park contains some significant areas of moist old-growth forest that hold the tallest trees in New South Wales. It is steep country and spectacularly beautiful, a place of rugged escarpments, waterfalls and magnificent giant white gums, *Eucalyptus nobilis*, rising above the forest canopy. The tallest white gum measured there is 79.22 metres, three metres taller than the Grandis tree [*Eucalyptus grandis*], the previous record holder at Bulahdelah.

But it is not to New South Wales or Tasmania that we should look to press Australia's claim to be the land of the world's tallest tree. In fact, Victoria has by far the most extraordinary historical tree records. Today, as in Tasmania, few mountain ash in Victoria exceed 90 metres. The state's current titleholder is a living tree at Wallaby Creek known as Big Ash One. It is 300 years old and still growing, with a measured height of 92.1 metres. Amebulas, in the Cumberland Tall Trees reserve nearby, exceeds 91 metres and the famous and majestic Ada Tree, in Powelltown Forest, is 71 metres tall. But go back in time and some astonishing measurements have been recorded: all of them relate to mountain ash and all of them are taller than Icarus Dream, the current record-holder for the species.

Critics of Australia's historic tall-tree claims often point out that in 1888 a fat cash reward of 100 pounds – a large sum in those days – was offered for the discovery of any tree measured at over 122 metres (400 feet in imperial measure). That reward was never claimed. What is less well recognised, as Al Carder realised on a more thorough reading of the history books, is that the reward was offered under conditions that made it very unlikely to be collected. First, the offer was made in the depths of winter and it applied only for a very short time. Next, the tree had to be measured by an accredited surveyor. Since axemen and 'paling splitters' had already been active for several decades in the Victorian forests, selectively taking the biggest and best trees, finding such tall trees demanded a long and arduous trek into wild country and at significant altitude. In turn, that required the additional skills of highly experienced bushmen, not only to guide the surveyor but to conduct an effective search within a likely area for the tallest trees and to come out alive. Understandably, there were few offers by suitable bushmen to lead such an uncertain enterprise.

The famous Ada Tree in Victoria

'As it was, only one expedition actually penetrated an area where *Eucalyptus regnans*, the tree of the mountains, thrived, and this excursion was rendered ineffectual by deep snow and cold,' Carder says. 'In addition, one of the party withdrew and another was overcome by the rigours of the journey.' Having reached the bitterly cold slopes of Mount Baw Baw, the group conducted one hasty search and managed to measure just one living tree before the appalling conditions made them turn tail and head for safety. The surveyor measured that tree – named the New Turkey Tree – at 99.4 metres. The reward offer soon expired but during kinder conditions a few years later, that same tree was felled for timber, reportedly along with much taller trees that were not measured. Another tree in the Mount Baw Baw area, known as the Neerim Giant, was measured in 1890 at 99 metres.

A shire engineer at Colac, in the Otway Ranges, reported a decade later that he had measured a fallen tree – described as a fine symmetrical specimen – near a beech

Mountain Ash reach prodigious heights on slender trunks

forest in Olangolah parish at just over 100 metres tall. The trunk diameter at its broken tip was 23 centimetres: using a reliable rule of thumb that every 2.54 centimetres of diameter equates with at least 0.75 metres in height, the engineer estimated that the original height of the Olangolah Tree was at least 106 metres.

Then in 1916 a surveyor named George Cornthwaite was working in mountain ash forest near Thorpdale when he came across a living monster, which he measured at 112.8 metres. When the Cornthwaite Tree was later felled for lumber the surveyor returned to the site and remeasured the fallen tree at 114.3 metres tall. You will note that this is some two metres taller than the Stratosphere Giant, and a metre taller than the so-called 'tallest tree of modern times', the Dyerville Giant.

Victoria's then State Botanical Officer, A.D. Hardy, later drew attention to a previously unknown report in 1911 by a licensed surveyor, G.W. Robinson, who had kept his personal forestry records from six decades earlier, during the 1850s in the Dandenong Ranges near Melbourne. The 'paling-splitters' were very active at the time supplying housing timber and Robinson had arranged to be notified whenever they came across a particularly tall tree. His notes revealed that every single tree he had measured exceeded 91 metres. The tallest was 104 metres to its dead tip, where the trunk diameter at the break was about fifteen centimetres, making its original height about 110 metres.

Robinson recalled that the big trees were cut first, and he had no doubt that 'some of the trees felled earlier would have measured quite some 400 feet [122 metres]'. He also gave an insight into the mindset of the paling-splitters, the men who actually downed and dismembered these stupendous trees with their axes and saws. 'Often when scrambling about over logs and fallen branches to measure a fallen giant, the splitters seemed to regard me with pity, as being a little daft,' Robinson wrote. Having explained to them that none other the Baron Sir Ferdinand von Mueller, Victoria's famous and much respected State Botanist in those early days, was anxious to have the measurements made, 'it only increased their pity, and they regarded us both as daft'.

Despite his international reputation as a diligent, painstaking and reputable scientist, von Mueller was, it must be said, a bit eccentric and a bit tree-mad (which only endears him to this author). He let all and sundry know of his passion for tall-tree measurements and made many himself, including a 122-metre whopper near the headwaters of the Yarra. But one of his informants, a government surveyor named David Boyle, topped that with an amazing measurement taken in 1862 on a fallen tree in a deep gully in the Dandenongs. It had a clean barrel for 92 metres and was 119.5 metres in all, up to the inevitable dieback break in its trunk. Based on the thickness of the break, its original living height would have been about 128 metres.

Von Mueller's early records include other Goliaths, but these are of uncertain reliability or based on hearsay. They include two mighty trees on the Black Spur range, one alive and measuring 128 metres and the other a fallen one measuring 146 metres. Another report from David Boyle was of a tree at Cape Otway alleged to be an incredible 158 metres tall, but Boyle did not measure it himself. As Al Carder argues, we cannot credit all these reports as being true, but neither can we dismiss them as figments of the imagination because they came from so many witnesses, from so many places and over such a long time.

But wait, there's one more – and it's a ripper. In 1982, the late Ken Simpendorfer, Special Projects Officer for the Forests Commission, Victoria, directed a search of official Victorian archives that turned up a long-forgotten but crucial report from more than a century earlier by an Inspector of State Forests, William Ferguson.

The report was written on 21 February 1872, and addressed to the then Assistant Commissioner of Lands and Surveys, Clement Hodgkinson. Ferguson was reporting back on his findings after being instructed to explore and inspect the watershed of one of the Yarra's tributaries, the Watts River. In his report he notes that the river flats and surrounding ranges boasted mountain ash trees in great number and of exceptional size. In no other forests had he seen such large trees, and his survey took him to places where woodcutters and paling-splitters had not yet penetrated. Ferguson wrote:

The Andromeda Reserve skyline in Tasmania: 100 trees of exceptional height

> Some places, where the trees are fewer and at a lower altitude, the timber
> is much larger in diameter, averaging 6 feet to 10 feet [1.8 to 3 metres] and
> frequently trees to 15 feet [4.5 metres] are met with on alluvial flats near
> the river. These trees average about ten per acre; their size, sometimes, is
> enormous. Many of the trees that have fallen through decay and by bush fires

measure 350 feet [106 metres] in length, with girth in proportion. In one instance I measured with the tape line one huge specimen that lay prostrate across a tributary of the Watts, and found it to be 435 feet [132.6 metres] from its roots to the top of the trunk. At 5 feet from the ground it measures 18 feet in diameter, and at the extreme end where it has broken in its fall, it is 3 feet in diameter. This tree has been much burnt by fire, and I fully believe that before it fell it must have been more than 500 feet high [152.4 metres]. As it now lies, it forms a complete bridge across a deep ravine.

This document was an amazing and truly important find. It is a first-hand official account from a highly credible and knowledgeable senior forester. What's more, it did not rely on estimation but a direct tape measurement made by him on a fallen tree. The intact part of the Ferguson Tree alone was 18.3 metres greater in height than the Stratosphere Giant. If the missing metre-thick portion of the mighty broken trunk is included, the Ferguson Tree leaves the current record-holder far behind, by some 38 metres. We're talking the Ozone Layer Giant here. It was as tall as a 45-storey skyscraper – truly incredible.

The tallest living mountain ash today has got a way to grow yet to reclaim the world title but new discoveries are being made all the time. The current record holder, Icarus Dream, was found while this book was in preparation and I wouldn't be surprised if a taller one has been found by the time you're reading this. This fabulous tree is well and truly alive but it's probably not going to grow any taller – in fact it's getting shorter – due to its advanced age.

Icarus Dream grows in the remarkable Andromeda Tall Trees Reserve in the Styx Valley of Tasmania, a 25-hectare reserve where about 100 trees are quite exceptional for their height. It is sobering to think that they might have been logged and the trees pulped for newsprint a few decades back, and the world would have been none the wiser.

Australian Newsprint Mills (ANM) had the logging concession for the area and in 1962 it sent in a team of three experienced forestry surveyors – L.D. Davey, R. Terry and J. Eagle – before felling got under way. The Andromeda Reserve was one of several small informal reserves declared as a result, in recognition of the outstanding height of the trees it contained. The team had measured more than a dozen trees of great height, and possibly more. But, for unknown reasons, the written records of their measurements were lost, so no heights and locations were known. Even though Andremoda Reserve is relatively small, it is so steep in places and so densely packed with mountain ash that finding and measuring even the tallest tree is a daunting exercise. The reserve is still surrounded by working forests. When I visited the site with Greens Senator Bob Brown I was shocked to see the reserve standing on one side of a deep gully that had been clearfelled on the other. From where we stood we could see the top of the towering Mount Tree, the former record-holder as tallest living tree at 96.5 metres.

It was knocked off its perch soon afterwards by one of its near neighbours, which, appropriately, was rediscovered and given its rightful crown by two of Australia's most dedicated lovers of tall trees, Tom Greenwood and Brett Mifsud. It is equally apt that Greenwood is our national tree-climbing champion – yes, they do have competitions – and a professional aborist. Mifsud's day job is teaching music, but tall and giant trees are a passion that consumes much of his spare time and most of the hard drive on his home computer.

Icarus Dream:
Australia's tallest tree
STYX VALLEY, TASMANIA

You can't write a book like this and not come across the name Mifsud in the record books, as the person who either discovered a certain tree or measured it. He is formally accredited by Forestry Tasmania as someone whose tree measurements are 'taken as gospel'. One whopper 85-metre mountain ash growing near Wayatinah, in Tasmania, is named after him, the Mifsud Tree. A likeable, generous young man, Brett Mifsud works long and hard, and at some personal risk, to identify and measure our outstanding trees. Not only that, but he freely shares his knowledge with others and keeps meticulous records.

Brett and I had talked on the phone and exchanged correspondence when I got an excited email from him in January 2005, shortly after he and Tom Greenwood had returned from a tree-hunting trip in Tasmania. They had been to the Andromeda Reserve to re-measure the Mount Tree, which Greenwood had once measured as 96.5 metres tall. (I hasten to add that they do not climb these trees with spikes, or do anything to damage them. They use a laser-guided instrument that looks like a pair of binoculars to get an approximate tree height from the ground. If they find a worthy contender, they fire a rope up to a suitably strong fork in the tree and abseil up, climbing only the top. From there, weighted measuring tapes can be lowered to the ground to verify the instrument reading.) Mifsud's email said:

Facing page:
Icarus Dream is 97
metres high

Great news. While Tom was fussing around trying to get a line up in the Mount Tree to recheck his old measurement, I went fossicking around the steep slopes of the Andromeda Reserve with Tom's Impulse [the radar instrument] as it's good at hitting the dead tops. At first I was fussing around

Brett Mifsud (above) and Tom Greenwood use lasers to measure tall trees, then climb them to verify the height

with a tree that seemed about 91 metres tall, and suspected no one else had measured it, then I zapped another top just 25 metres to the left of the first tree, and it appeared 5 metres taller than the first tree. The slope is very steep and I was getting figures between 95.5 to 96 metres. Once we'd climbed the tree and done a ground survey we got the figure of 97.0 metres, over 318 feet in the old language, the world's tallest known hardwood!

The new champion was not just tall but broad in the butt as well, with girth of 9.1 metres at chest height. The tip of its crown was dead and Greenwood and Mifsud reckoned that when those branches were alive it would have been two to three metres taller. 'Perhaps we were climbing a tree that once topped 100 metres. I have called the new tree Icarus Dream . . . We also climbed the Mount Tree later on that day and it had shrunk to 96.1m, so I climbed the two tallest eucalypts in the one day!'

Greenwood later told me the climb was well worth the effort, with a spectacular vantage point over the scene below. Beneath Icarus Dream the slope falls away steeply into a moist gully:

The other trees look very different from above and it's odd looking down their trunks instead of up. Even though its top six to eight metres is dead wood it's quite a healthy tree and it's sent out a lot of new growth from its

trunk since the area nearby was logged years ago. Beneath me I could see some sassafras, tree ferns and lower down myrtles and wattles. It was lovely. I could also see the Mount Tree, just 145 metres away, but for me the real excitement was getting that measurement. You're very unlikely to find a tree that tall these days.

Measuring tall trees is not for the faint-hearted especially when their tops are often dead and decaying

The pair are the first to acknowledge that Icarus Dream was actually rediscovered. When they later searched around its base they found a rotted wooden stake with a metal disc marked with the number 324. Subsequent inquiries have shown that this indicated a height of 324 feet (98.75 metres) estimated in 1962 by the ANM survey team led by Ron Davey. It would appear that Icarus Dream has shrunk since then.

But it is no midget. It would overshadow three blue whales – at 30 metres in length, the largest animal that ever lived – stacked head to tail beside it. Its tip is twenty metres higher than the light towers at the Melbourne Cricket Ground. If it grew at Circular Quay it would look down on the traffic on the Sydney Harbour Bridge, or on the highest sail on the Sydney Opera House. In London, it would be taller than the famous Clock Tower that houses Big Ben. If it grew in New York it would soar above the Statue of Liberty and you'd have to ride the lift 32 floors up the Empire State Building before you drew level with its top.

After the ravages of logging and bushfires in earlier times, no old mountain ash trees of such great height exist these days in Victoria but some relatively young ones there do have very impressive dimensions. One day Brett Mifsud took me for a drive through some of the country he knows and loves best in the Black Spur Range near Healesville. And spectacular it is, too. The mountain ash forests there are

extraordinary, whole cities of living green skyscrapers wearing fluffy slippers – the giant tree ferns that grow on the forest floor. All human activity there is strictly limited and tightly controlled because it is part of the catchment for Melbourne's drinking water supply, one of the cleanest in the world. It is one of the most beautiful forest scenes in Australia, like being in a vast cathedral.

What is also remarkable about these forests, though, is that there are almost no old trees. Look closely and you notice that the trees are all of similar height and diameter, allowing for local habitat and genetic variations. What you see there, Mifsud told me, is a result of the appalling 1939 Black Friday bushfires, when these and many other forests went up in a deadly inferno. From the ashes of the fires sprang vast numbers of saplings from the seed rained down by the parent trees in their final act before they died. After one bushfire, an estimated 2.5 million mountain ash seedlings sprang up in a single hectare. They gradually muscle each other out in intense competition, until only about 40 per hectare reach maturity. To succeed they must grow very fast in their youth. Being 'crown-shy' as well – meaning that they

The ash forests in the Black Spur Range near Melbourne are almost all regrown from the 1939 Black Friday fires

don't like to touch their neighbours – their best option is to go straight up as fast as they can, without wasting energy on branches and big crowns. Only now, almost 70 years after Black Friday, do these mountain ash trees have substantial upper branches and significant crowns. Many were 60 metres tall, some had passed 70 metres and a special few had already climbed to 80 metres: that's a growth rate of more than a metre a year, sustained for almost seven decades straight.

But Mifsud could go one better. He took me to another place not far away, the location of which I'll keep quiet. We passed through tranquil farmland then turned down a winding dirt road along a small valley with paddocks petering out into bush. We passed a final farmhouse, crossed a ford over a creek and were suddenly on a forest track, back in mountain ash country.

In no time the car had crunched to a halt. 'Here we are,' said Brett. 'Follow me. And watch out for leeches.' We'd already had a taste of those that day, or they of us. We plunged into the undergrowth beneath another tall stand of trees, this time probably from the class of '26. The slope behind us was steep but the gully floor was levelling out when we came to a stop. Brett put his laser rangefinder to his eyes and peered up. 'That's them,' he said, passing the instrument to me and indicating three great beanpoles in front of us. I took a bead on the highest branches I could single out. All three were nudging 85 metres, with the tallest over 86 metres. I was amazed. These trees were mere teenagers and yet they were already five metres taller that any tree in New South Wales. Brett grinned. He had been monitoring these guys for some time and they were still growing strong. Protected deep in their gully in good soil beside a creek, they had everything going for them. Brett was excited and so was I. Would these be the very trees to outgrow Icarus Dream and bring the height records back to Victoria within our lifetime? Would they exceed 100 metres one day? And, oh my, would they power on to snatch back the world record from the North American coast redwoods? It was a lovely moment to share, a hopeful dream to nurture for the future. Mifsud said he called them the Bunjil's Spears.

Bunjil's Spears: all over 85 metres tall and still growing

Later I learned who Bunjil was, when I read a story told by Carolyn Briggs, a Boonerwrung elder, at a special Reconciliation Assembly of the Parliament of Victoria, on 31 May 2000. Among the original Kulin inhabitants of this land, Bunjil was the creator and spiritual leader of the people, who appeared as an eagle. A story told about him is that at one time the people were fighting amongst each other, neglecting their duties and the land. The sea became angry and started rising, threatening to flood their country. Frightened, they sought help from Bunjil. He made them agree to mend their ways and respect him and his laws. Only then did Bunjil walk out into the sea, with his spear held high, and command the sea to stop rising.

Big, bigger . . . biggest?

Other great
Australian trees,
past and present

The Transportation Tree

SYDNEY, NEW SOUTH WALES

In 1849 notices appeared around Sydney announcing:

> ### THE
> ## CONVICT SHIP
> ### HAS ARRIVED!
>
> **T**HE GREAT MEETING will be held on the CIRCULAR WHARF, TO-DAY, at Noon, to Protest against the Landing of the Convicts.
>
> The Chair will be taken by Robert Lowe, Esq., the Member for the City.
>
> Let all places of business be closed!
>
> Let every man be at his post!   9600

The ship *Hashemy* – the last convict ship to reach Sydney – was met by the fury of the anti-transportation movement. Rallying in the rain around a large pine tree in Bridge Street, between 4000 and 5000 Sydneysiders turned out to hear speakers denounce transportation. Robert Lowe – whom Manning Clark described as 'an albino who was riven to spite and malice to compensate for all the humiliations he had suffered at boarding school in England' – was greeted with vigorous applause when he denounced Great Britain for tipping its moral filth into New South Wales and for polluting the city with a floating hell.

For a time, there was hot-blooded talk of storming Government House and pressuring Governor FitzRoy to order the *Hashemy* back out to sea. In the end, according to the *Sydney Morning Herald*, the crowd kept its head and dispersed quietly. A deputation to FitzRoy won a compromise, where some convicts were landed but sent far from Sydney, while the rest sailed on to Moreton Bay to provide cheap labour for eager squatters there. The pine became known as the Transportation Tree and was conserved and protected by railings for three more decades until it began to decay and was felled to make way for a street expansion.

The Cairns Fig Tree
CAIRNS, QUEENSLAND

For more than a century a huge fig tree grew in Abbott Street. It was said to be quite large even when Cairns was first surveyed in the 1870s. It was much admired and photographed but controversy dogged its days. It blocked the traffic and grew to consume half the roadway until it was more than twenty metres high and seven metres in diameter. It wasn't easy to live with, since it was also a roosting place for hundreds of birds, including ibises and egrets, which decorated the tree and anything below it with white patches. When it was finally removed – in spite of protests – in August 1953 to let traffic flow more freely, it took the equivalent of three men working for a forty-hour week to do the job. Another giant felled in the name of progress.

The O'Reilly Tree
PICTON, WESTERN AUSTRALIA

This large gum tree – also known as Moondyne's Tree – grew somewhere near Picton, in the south-west. There was a romantic tale attached to it and to the man it was named after, the writer John Boyle O'Reilly (1844–90). In 1865, the staunchly nationalistic Irishman joined the secret rebel society known as the Fenians, who were plotting the overthrow of British rule in Ireland. O'Reilly was later arrested, tried and sentenced to twenty years imprisonment. After two years in English jails, he was sent on board a convict ship to Australia, arriving at Fremantle in 1869. He was soon put to work in a road gang, building a road between Bunbury and Vasse. His good behaviour won favour with his overseer and he was given trusted administrative tasks.

One early biography – *The Life of John Boyle O'Reilly*, by J.J. Roche, published in 1891 – described the tree as a handsome, well-formed gum of substantial proportions, which the foreman of the road gang had marked one day for felling. O'Reilly – a man of poetic passions – pleaded strongly for it to be spared and, when his request was refused, took the matter personally to the district commandant. The official's wife went herself to see the tree; she, too, greatly admired it and the tree was spared. 'Thus the imperial word was turned from its course and a grand work of nature stands in Western Australia's forests as a monument to the convict poet,' wrote Roche.

O'Reilly's subsequent life and adventures were remarkable. His early escape from

Australia involved an extraordinary voyage on longboats and whaling ships – involving much subterfuge, treachery and good fortune – and saw O'Reilly land eventually in the United States, where fellow Irish exiles embraced him. He settled in Boston, where he became a news reporter (and eventually editor): his first major assignment was to cover the Fenians' 1870 New York convention. He came to reject militancy but still campaigned vigorously and wrote copiously in favour of Irish independence. In 1875 he helped to mastermind the daring and now legendary plot for the successful rescue of six other Fenians still serving time in Western Australia, aboard a purpose-bought whaling ship, *Catalpa*. Over the years O'Reilly wrote several collections of poetry and in 1880 penned a novel, *Moondyne*, based on his convict days.

Here the plot thickens: Moondyne was said to be the Aboriginal name for the rugged Darling Range, east of Perth. The O'Reilly Tree's alternative name of Moondyne's Tree refers to a colourful local bushman named Joseph Johns, an ex-convict bushranger known as Moondyne Joe. His life and times are almost the equal of O'Reilly's for drama, with his remarkable fugitive escapades wearing a kangaroo-skin cape and possum-fur slippers. The central character of O'Reilly's book was called Moondyne Joe. The identity of the tree itself, where it stood and who saved it, is a matter of some doubt. One account had it that it was not O'Reilly at all but another convict who interceded on the tree's behalf. Another claimed it was not the Picton gum but a most unusually shaped tuart tree near Bunbury that was known as both the Kite Tree and the Horseshoe Tree. In the end it is a wonderful colourful story and the questions surrounding the two trees are of little consequence: the tuart tree was later cut down and the gum tree was felled in 1951 after officials met and decided it was so decayed as to be a public danger.

Paddy Hannan's Tree
KALGOORLIE, WESTERN AUSTRALIA

This tree marks the spot where Paddy Hannan first found gold in 1893 in Kalgoorlie. The kurrajong tree is in a fenced-in area, with a memorial plaque, on Outridge Terrace near the top of Hannan Street. Originally a pepper tree was ceremonially planted there in 1897; Hannan was at the function but modestly declined to do the planting. When the tree decayed in 1929, the kurrajong was planted in its place.

The Tree of Knowledge
DARWIN, NORTHERN TERRITORY

This is the 'other' Tree of Knowledge, not the one at Barcaldine in Queensland, but a massive banyan tree in Darwin that was once a focal point for public gatherings, a landmark where people meet, and even a mailing address. It was ideally located for its purpose, near the wharf and railway station, and outside a pub. It escaped serious damage when the area was devastated by Japanese bombing during World War II, but never again had the same status after rebuilding took place. In the late 1960s and early 1970s a community campaign to save it was successful, and it was incorporated into the Darwin Civic Centre development. The tree was heritage-listed in 1994. The Northern Territory Library logo is based on this tree, a banyan encompassed by a half-circle dome.

The long-lived banyans achieve an extraordinary spread by putting down aerial roots from their branches to support their lateral limbs, resulting in a dramatic tangle of vertical props that invite you to sit in the shade and let the imagination wander. Aboriginal people traditionally stripped the bark of the prop roots to make string. The bark was torn into strips and dried in the sun, then the fibres were entwined by rubbing them on the thigh; among other things, carry bags, armbands and decorative jewellery were made with it.

Other great Australian trees

The Banyan Tree

GOVE, NORTHERN TERIRTORY

At the Alcan Alumina Plant at Gove, also in the Northern Territory, is another exceptional banyan. When the plant was being built a Yolngu elder, Mungurrawuy Yunupingu, stood in front of the banyan armed with an axe – not to cut the tree down but to ward off an advancing bulldozer sent to clear the site. With him was his young son, Galarrwuy Yunupingu, who went on to become chairman of the Northern Land Council and an Australian of the Year. He later recalled his father's passion for the site and being urged to protect the tree as the home of the spiritual guardian of the rainforest that once surrounded it. In his excellent book *Tree Stories*, Peter Solness relates Galarrwuy Yunupingu's memory of his father's confrontation with the bulldozer: 'He told the driver to tell his boss not to damage this tree … My father was amazing. He could comprehend what the development meant so he said, "Leave my tree".' And they did: the site plan was altered to relocate a proposed workshop and warehouse, and the refinery was built around the banyan. There's another great specimen in the central Queensland city of Rockhampton, in the Botanic Gardens. Planted in the 1870s, it has grown into a giant with a foliage spread reportedly close to 100 metres.

The tree they built a refinery around

The Wishing Tree

SYDNEY, NEW SOUTH WALES

In their passion to create a grand formal landscape around the first Government House in Sydney, Governor and Mrs Macquarie planted many imposing trees during their tenure from 1810 to 1821. One of them was a Norfolk Island pine, raised from seed by Mrs Macquarie herself. When it grew too large for her garden, it was transplanted in 1815 to the Botanic Gardens, to a round garden bed on the eastern where it became known as the Wishing Tree and went on to be one of Sydney's best-known trees. For reasons that remain obscure, young ladies of the colony settled on this tree to revive a much older European practice of performing certain rites to summon up the mystical spirits supposed to dwell in some trees. The virile growth and towering symmetry of this tree clearly had that certain something that fostered a faith in it. The practice was to rap your knuckles lightly on a tree and make a wish – said to be the origin of the superstitious expression 'touch wood' – or to circle around it in a prescribed way. In this case, young Sydney women circled the Wishing Tree three times forwards then three times backwards. This charming ritual was played out countless times over the ensuing decades as the tree grew to an outstanding height on the skyline.

And old photo of the Wishing Tree: young women circled it three times and 'touched wood' for luck in love

After 120 years it became apparent that the pine was decaying with age so a new Norfolk Island pine was planted nearby by Lady Hore-Ruthven (later Lady Gowrie) on 27 July 1935. A decade later, in September 1945, the original pine was too far gone and had to be removed: parts were preserved for posterity and some of the wood was made into toys. The replacement Wishing Tree did not achieve the same popularity. Soon after it was planted a storm damaged its crown – hardly a sign of good fortune – and although it thrives today it will never achieve the columnar grandeur of its predecessor. At the site where it grew, however, a statue of a female figure now bears a plaque that reads 'I wish': visitors still place flowers on it. Directly behind it is growing one of the first Wollemi pines to be planted outside its ancient Blue Mountains grove (unfortunately still caged unattractively for its own protection at the time of writing). Perhaps in time its ancient origins will have the mystique to attract a new generation of followers.

Other great Australian trees

Mrs Macquarie's Tree
PARRAMATTA, NEW SOUTH WALES

Elizabeth Macquarie's name will endure far into the future for its association with the point known as Mrs Macquarie's Chair, which juts out into Sydney Harbour from the Domain. It was her favourite place to sit and take in the spectacular view of the harbour and the comings and goings of its ships. You can still see the steps and the bench seat carved for her into a sandstone outcrop, with an inscription that marks the place.

Far less well known is that when she resided at the Governor's estate at Parramatta she had another favourite vantage point in a treehouse. It was a tall gum tree, around the trunk of which a spiral stairway was fixed to give access to a platform built for her near its top. From here, Mrs Macquarie could take in an expansive vista of the surrounding countryside, her landscaping efforts and the settlement that was quickly growing there. A newspaper report in 1849 mentioned simply that the tree would soon be removed. It is thought to have been cut down in 1860 to make way for a railway line through the park. No trace of Mrs Macquarie's tree remains today.

Andrew Petrie's Tree
NEAR BRISBANE, QUEENSLAND

The Petrie family were pioneers in the Brisbane region, arriving in 1837 before free settlement began. Andrew Petrie had come to Australia in 1831 from Scotland as a builder and played a significant tole in the city's early days. Hi s son Tom was well known for running away from home at fifteen and living briefly with Aborigines, for whom he became a friend, interpreter and defender. Both Andrew and Tom are said to have blazed many trees to guide new settlers, and Andrew is credited with 'discovering' the amazing bunya pine, with its massive seed cones. But one individual tree in particular was associated with his name, a landmark eucalypt at the summit of Mount Petrie, near Brisbane. It was inscribed 'A. Petrie, 1838', and a drawing of it appeared in the 1904 biography *Tom Petrie's Reminiscences of Early Queensland*. Sadly, in view of its great historical significance, that tree was felled to make way for a survey point. A search was made in 1896 to retrieve and conserve the inscribed trunk, but no trace of it was to be seen.

The Queen of the Colonies Tree

CALOUNDRA, QUEENSLAND

A large pandanus palm once grew by the sea on the north coast of Brisbane. A cryptic inscription on its trunk read: 'Queen of the Colonies, 1863'. The inscription referred to the immigrant ship of that name, which dropped anchor to let a burial party go ashore when a young female passenger died from an illness as it approached Moreton Bay in 1863. She was buried near the palm on Cape Moreton, with her husband watching in tears. The tragedy was compounded when the burial party, returning to the ship, was caught unawares by a freshening breeze; their boat capsized and the grieving widower was drowned. The survivors were able to reach shore again, but the worsening weather meant that the captain of the *Queen of the Colonies* could not reach them. It was two weeks before an overland party from Brisbane could rescue them, by which time the survivors were in a 'pitiable' condition due to hunger and exposure. A plaque on Moffat Headland marks the event.

The palm was wrecked during a storm sometime during the 1940s, but the section of its trunk with the inscription was salvaged and placed in the care of the (now Royal) Queensland Historical Society, at Newstead House, in Brisbane, where it occasionally goes on display. It is a modest piece of wood about 30 centimetres long, and the inscription is only partly visible.

The R.R. Mac Tree

CENTRAL QUEENSLAND

In the 1850s, the pastoralist Robert Ramsey Mackenzie carved a tree with his 'R.R. Mac' blaze while exploring for new grazing country in central Queensland. A few years later, in 1859, the explorer William Landsborough came across the tree and was inspired by the inscription to name the nearby watercourse Aramac Creek. In due course, Mackenzie became Premier of Queensland and was knighted, while the creek gave its name to a town and then a shire. Queensland boasts at least two other geographical place names inspired by initials blazed on trees: L Creek and M Creek can both be found in the Gulf Country. The tiny township of Canterbury in north-western Queensland was known by locals as JC, in reference to an early pioneer John Costello carving his initials on a tree 56 miles west of Windorah. In Victoria, there's a town called W Tree – postcode 3885 – so named for a prominent tree that was left W-shaped by storm damage.

Father Woods' Tree

SOUTH AUSTRALIA

Beside the road between Penola and Naracoorte is perhaps the only tree in Australia named after a parish priest. An accomplished geologist and mineralogist as well as a man of the cloth, Father Tenison Woods was ordained in the Catholic Church in 1857 and put in charge of a huge parish that extended tens of thousands of square kilometres across south-eastern South Australia and western Victoria. He served his flock devotedly for a decade, travelling by horseback between communities and following his love of science and of God.

The Father Woods Tree marks the place where, in the absence of a church, his parishioners in that district would gather to hear him preach and hold services. Local legend has it that he also did some writing beneath the tree, which he once described as 'a broom to brush sin from the south-east'. In 1867 he transferred back to Adelaide as secretary to the Bishop and director-general of Catholic education. Among his many friends was Mother Mary McKillop, who founded the teaching Order of St Joseph in South Australia in 1866. Woods went on to serve with distinction elsewhere in both science and the church. He died in 1889 and was buried at Waverley Cemetery in Sydney.

Lacking a church, Father Woods held services beneath this tree

235

The Halfway Tree
WESTERN AUSTRALIA

Also known as the Six-Mile Tree, this old eucalypt on the Stirling Highway between Perth and Fremantle was the handover point where mailmen from the two centres used to meet to swap mailbags and gossip. A plaque erected there in 1936 claimed that these meetings took place 'from the earliest days of the colony up to 1867'. When the road was widened in the 1930s, the tree was felled.

The Pioneers' Tree
LEETON, NEW SOUTH WALES

By all accounts this was a wonderful old kurrajong in the centre of the town, a local landmark that once sheltered the travellers and stockmen who met and camped beneath its boughs. Locals say it was already old when the town was established in 1914, to a design by American architect Walter Burley Griffin, who had recently designed the city of Canberra. Like Canberra, Leeton was purpose-built – in this case as part of the development of the Murrumbidgee Irrigation Area – with a circular design at its core and four street precincts fanning out from the town centre. Being a unique marker of the area's history, the kurrajong became known as the Pioneers' Tree and, as a plaque attached to it in 1939 noted, it 'stood here long before the Murrumbidgee Irrigation Areas were envisaged, and in due course Kurrajong Avenue and the town itself were designed and grew up around it'. Sadly, this distinctive tree was later struck by lightning, killed and removed. A replacement kurrajong was planted in its stead, but that was also destroyed a few years ago when an out-of-control car crashed into it. Subsequent traffic changes have meant that all that remains today is the name of the avenue and the plaque.

The tree that housed a family

The stumps left behind after the felling of massive trees in the Gippsland region of Victoria later found notoriety for the inventive ways that settlers employed them. One formed a kind of tunnel, through which carts passed on a track. Others had roofs built over them and served a variety of practical purposes as makeshift buildings. One became a kiln for drying hops. Another, with an internal diameter of more than five metres, was fitted with a timber roof and used as a milking-shed for a dairy. It later found a new lease of life as a modest church that could accommodate some twenty worshippers. Later still, it became a school room and then a stable that housed five horses.

More than a few hardy souls made temporary homes in tree stumps and hollows, and few such stories can surpass that of Johann Friedrich Herbig. Like many Germans before and after him, he left his homeland in search of opportunity and a new life in South Australia's Barossa Valley, now justly famous for its wine.

Herbig arrived from Bremen aboard the ship *Wilhelmine* in October 1855. A tailor by trade, he soon found work as a farm labourer at Black Springs (now Springton, about 60 kilometres north-east of Adelaide) but was confronted immediately with the harsh reality that trees were in short supply and so was timber for housing. Those with the time and the assets to spare could afford to use stone for their houses, but new chums and newlyweds often simply lived in make-do huts assembled from whatever materials they could fit to the purpose.

Friedrich Herbig worked hard and saved hard and soon had enough money to purchase his own land in an arrangement that let him pay off the sum over a number of

Freidrich Herbig's descendants saved his tree and gathered for a 150th reunion of his tree house

years. But he still needed somewhere to live, and preferably somewhere cheap. To his rescue came a huge river red gum with a massive bulging buttressed base. By dint of time and circumstance, the tree's centre had been naturally hollowed. The tree is now thought to be between 300 and 500 years old and it has been suggested that its peculiar base was either the result of an old lightning strike or of Aboriginal campfires. Indeed, Friedrich may not have been the first person to be faced with a decision to occupy this tree for lack of other shelter.

The following year, among the new German arrivals on the ship *Vesta* was a young woman from Hamburg, Anna Caroline Rattey, who later moved to the Barossa Valley and caught Friedrich's eye. Love blossomed, as love does, and after they were married in 1858 they both lived in Herbig's tree. Love soon bore fruit as well, with their first child – Johann August –born there in 1859, and a second son the following year. With the family expanding, even this mighty tree wasn't large enough to accommodate the Herbigs, so in 1860 they built a timber hut about 400 metres away, then a stone cottage a few years later.

The couple made the final payment on their land in 1867, by which time they had a new house. As their family grew, so did their landholdings and business interests: ultimately they owned 400 hectares of land and produced sixteen children. A year after celebrating his silver wedding anniversary, Friedrich was killed in an accident and was buried at the Friedenberg cemetery. He had taught himself English from a German-English dictionary but Caroline still spoke little English and could not read or write. Despite this, she successfully brought up her remaining children. Before she died at age 87, in 1927, she had witnessed the birth of many grandchildren and the deaths of seven of her own children. After the Herbigs moved out, others later used the tree as a home as well. In the 1920s, it was still in use as a place to serve lunches on sale days for a nearby stockyard.

In 1968 descendants of the Herbig family formed a memorial trust and bought the land containing the tree. Some 900 of them, including 51 grandchildren, gathered there on the 150th anniversary of Friedrich's first occupation of the tree for a commemorative celebration.

State-by-state list of trees

Sources

Anon., *Think Trees Grow Trees*, Australian Government Publishing Service, Canberra, 1985

Anon., The Proclamation Tree, Celebrate WA website www.celebratewa.com.au/Events/view.asp?DetailsID=89

Anon., *York Park North ACT*, National Trust Endangered Places List 2004, October, 2006 www.nationaltrust.org.au/ep04/documents/YorkParkNorthACT.pdf

Archer, Michael & Beale, Bob, *Going Native: living in the Australian environment*, Hodder Headline, Sydney, 2004

Ashton, Ralph (ed), *Tarkine*, Allen and Unwin, Sydney, 2004

Bail, Murray, *Eucalyptus*, Text Publishing, 1998

Beale, Bob, *Tree of Life*, The Bulletin, 25 June, 2003

Beale, Bob & Fray, Peter, *The Vanishing Continent: Australia's degraded environment*, Hodder and Stoughton, Sydney, 1990

Bonyhady, Tim, *The Colonial Earth*, Melbourne University Press, Melbourne, 2002

Brooker, Ian & Kleinig, David, *Eucalyptus*, Reed New Holland, Sydney, 2004

Brooks, A.E., *Tree Wonders of Australia*, Heinemann, Melbourne, 1964

Carder, Al, *Forest Giants of the World, Past and Present*, Fitzwarren Publishing, 1995

Carstenz, Jan, *Journal*, pp. 41–42, 1623 www.kb.nl/galerie/australie/2/full%20text.pdf#search=%22Jan%20Carstenz%20journal%22

Clark, Manning, *A Short History of Australia*, Penguin Books, Melbourne, 1988

Collins, David, *An Account of the English Colony in New South Wales, with Remarks on the Dispositions, Customs, Manners, etc., of the Native Inhabitants of that country, Vol 1*, Orig. 1798. Brian H. Fletcher, (ed.), Sydney, A. H. and Reed, A. W. with the Royal Australian Historical Society, 1975, pp. 5–6

Dargavel, John, 'Trees age and memories change in the Avenues of Honour and Remembrance', in *Australia's Ever-changing Forests IV: Proceedings of the Fourth National Conference on Australian Forest History*, Dargavel, John and Libbis, Brenda (eds), Centre for Resource and Environmental Studies, Australian National University, Canberra, 1999

Dupuis, Jean, *Marvellous World of Trees*, Abbey Library, London, 1976

East, Ronald (ed), *The Gallipoli Diary of Sergeant Lawrence*, Melbourne, 1983, www.anzacsite.gov.au/2visiting/walk_08lonepine.html

Edwards, Geoffrey, *Giant – ancient and historic trees*, Geelong Gallery (exhibition catalogue), 2003

French, Alison, *Seeing the Centre: the art of Albert Namatjira 1902–1959*, National Gallery of Australia, Canberra, 2002

Furphy, Joseph, *Such is Life*, Globusz Publishing, (e-book) www.globusz.com/ebooks/SuchIsLife/00000012.htm

Gray, Alan, *Conclusions on El Grande (eucalyptus regnans)*, report to The Wilderness Society, April 2003 www.wilderness.org.au/campaigns/forests/tasmania/elgrand_03/

Grolier Society of Australia, *The Australian Encyclopaedia*, Halstead Press, Sydney, 1963

www.guinessworldrecords.com/content_pages/record.asp?recordid=47342

Hay, Ashley, *Gum: the story of eucalypts and their champions*, Duffy and Snellgrove, Sydney, 2002

Howell, Jocelyn & Benson, Doug, *Sydney's Bushland: more than meets the eye*, Royal Botanic Gardens Sydney, Sydney, 2000

King, Jonathan & Bowers, Michael, *Gallipoli: Untold Stories*, Doubleday, Sydney, 2005

Leader-Elliott, Lyn & Iwanicki, Iris, *Heritage of the Birdsville and Strzlecki Tracks*, Report for the South Australian and Commonwealth Governments, Historical Research Pty Ltd, Adelaide, 2002

Lindenmayer, David & Beaton, Esther, *Life in the Tall Eucalypt Forests*, Reed New Holland, Sydney, 2000

Macarthur, John, quoted in *Guidebook, Elizabeth Farm 1793*, Historic Houses Trust www.hht.net.au/museums/ef/guidebook

Marchant-James, Ruth, *The Foundation of Perth*, Celebrate WA website www.celebratewa.com.au/Events/view.asp?DetailsID=83

Mattingley, Christobel, *King of the Wilderness: The Life of Deny King*, Text Publishing, Melbourne, 2001

Murgatroyd, Sarah, *The Dig Tree*, Text Publishing, Melbourne, 2002

Pakenham, Thomas, *Remarkable Trees of the World*, Weidenfeld and Nicolson, London, 2002

Perry, Dulcie, *The Place of Waters: A history of the first fifty years of Glenelg*, The Author, Adelaide, 1985

Pyne, Stephen, *Burning Bush: a fire history of Australia*, Henry Holt, New York, 1991

Register of Historic Places and Objects, Professional Historians Association (NSW), Inc, NSW Heritage Register (SHI number 4671012) www.phansw.org.au/Rohpo/brachychiton.pdf#search=%22dooligah%20and%20kuritja%22

Robinson, Les, *Field Guide to the Native Plants of Sydney*, Kangaroo Press, Sydney, 1997

Rolls, Eric, *Visions of Australia: Impressions of the Landscape*, Lothian Books, Sydney, 2002

Sinclair, Paul, *The Murray: a river and its people*, Melbourne University Press, Melbourne, 2001

Solness, Peter, *Tree Stories*, Chapter and Verse, Sydney, 1999

Morton Spencer, Gwen & Ure Smith, Sam (eds), *Australian Treescapes*, Ure Smith Miniature Series 7, 1950

Stubbs, B. J. and Saenger, P., *The Investigator Tree: Eighteenth century inscriptions, or twentieth century misinterpretations?* Burke Shire Council website (originally published in the Journal of the Royal Historical Society of Queensland, August 1996) www.burkeshirecouncil.com/sweers_island/investigator_tree.htm

Thomas, Peter, *Trees: Their Natural History*, Cambridge University Press, Cambridge, 2000

UK Department of Culture, Media and Sport, *The Elfin Oak of Kensington Gardens is listed*, (media release, 19 December, 1997) www.prnewswire.co.uk/cgi/news/release?id=24559

Wandin, James, address to the Parliament of Victoria, May 2000 www.parliament.vic.gov.au/windowintime/views/showview.cfm?viewid=0

Webster, Sally, *Harold Cazneaux Photographs – The Catalogue*, exhibition catalogue, National Library of Australia/Historic Houses Trust of New South Wales, Canberra, 1997 www.nla.gov.au/exhibitions/caz/cat.html

Woodford, James, *The Wollemi Pine: the incredible discovery of a living fossil from the age of the dinosaurs*, Text Publishing, Melbourne, 2000

Picture Credits

Unless otherwise stated, photographs of trees have been taken by Bob Beale. All tree silhouettes throughout are by Phil Campbell and Bob Beale.

Page 4: Peter Dombrovskis, Myrtle tree in rainforest at Mount Anne, southwest Tasmania, 1984, nla.pic-an24358043, National Library of Australia. Courtesy of and copyright Liz Dombrovskis, West Wind Press.

Page 6: Nicholas Caire, The tree and the house built out of it, nla.pic-an3143304, National Library of Australia.

Page 13: Jeff Carter, Broadaxemen 2, Telegraph Point, New South Wales,1955, nla.pic-vn3102864, National Library of Australia. Courtesy of and copyright Jeff Carter.

Page 46: John Flynn, Unidentified man climbing a tree, nla.pic-an24377744, National Library of Australia.

Page 52: Joseph Lycett, Aborigine climbing a tree by cutting steps in the trunk, nla.pic-an2962715-s4, National Library of Australia.

Page 71: River red gum, courtesy of Andrew Chapman.

Page 82: William Strutt, Portrait of Robert O'Hara Burke, nla.pic-an3874535, National Library of Australia.

Page 93: Tree of knowledge, courtesy of Newspix (photographer Bruce Long).

Page 107: Ballarat Avenue of Honour, courtesy of Dan Reid.

Page 115: Mrs Ivy Brookes planting a tree, in memory of Alfred Deakin, in the Prime Minister's Corridor at Faulconbridge, N.S.W., 17 August, 1936, nla.ms-ms1540-19-550, National Library of Australia.

Page 118 (top): G. C. Fenton, Proclamation tree at Glenelg, South Australia, nla.pic-an5836948, National Library of Australia.

Page 118 (bottom): Group of unidentified children at the Old Gum Tree, Glenelg: part of South Australian and other AIM [Australian Inland Mission] scenes used by Rev. F.H. Patterson, nla.pic-an24220219, National Library of Australia.

Page 141: Frank Hurley, Gloucester Tree look-out, near Pemberton, Western Australia, nla.pic-an23182145, National Library of Australia.

Page 185: Arthur Groom, Mr Bob Gunther, manager of Monkira, and the giant coolabah, 46 feet around the girth Queensland, 1952, nla.pic-an23182114, National Library of Australia.

Page 188: Arthur Groom, Don McKenzie, the Monkira head-stockman on the left, is over 80 years old Queensland, 1952, nla.pic-an23165362, National Library of Australia.

Pages 10, 62, 79, 155, 230, 237: courtesy of Peter Solness.

Pages 61, 97, 98, 103, 124, 229: courtesy of iStock.

Pages 136–7 and 222–3: Royal Botanic Gardens Melbourne, courtesy of Greg Elms.

Page 194, 199, 217–9: courtesy of Brett Mifsud.

Acknowledgements

Special thanks go to Brett Mifsud – tall-tree hunter extraordinaire – for his enthusiasm, willing assistance and unsung exertions for the common good. Thanks, too, to Tom Greenwood – tree-climber extraordinaire – for his lofty ambitions. Doug Benson gave generously of his time and shared his great knowledge of trees. Ken Hill also enthused me about eucalypts and informed me about the Wollemi pine. Ashley Hay shared a passion for trees and some wonderful stories. Brett Mifsud, Rick Stevens, Steve Preece and Janice Latham all helped with photographs and technical advice. Lis Sterel fed, watered and inspired me, listened to and advised me while writing, and tolerated many distractions and diversions to look at and talk about trees. Mike Archer encouraged me and provided thoughtful feedback and advice. Debbie Deseraux of Monkira Station went out of her way to help me. Thanks also to Geelong Art Gallery; John Dargavel; Robert Boden; Phillip Law; Bob Brown; James Woodford; Sue Hines; Tara Wynne; Andrea McNamara; Rosie Fitzgibbon, a fine copy editor; Friends of the Botanic Gardens, Sydney; botanic gardeners of many kinds in Sydney, Melbourne, Hobart and Geelong. Thanks, finally, to the late Billy White, my all-too-brief childhood friend and blood brother who taught me to see the bush with new eyes.